Advanced Praise for *Leading with Cultural Humility*

"Lyna addresses unconscious bias through sharing real life examples and dispelling the narrative that only bad people with ill intent have bias. At the end of the chapter, she makes the learning actionable in her "Takeaways" and "Call to Learn". I would highly recommend this as a DEI read for those who are new to the work and a refresher for those who have been in the movement for some time."

Angel Uddin
Director - Equity, Diversity, & Inclusion
University of Minnesota
Minneapolis, MN

As a leader, and continuing to move diversity, equity, inclusion, and belonging work forward at my organization, there will be tough conversations that need to be had and this book gives actionable tools to help me navigate through those challenging conversations. Lyna offers a great resource here!

Dr. Leanne Rogstad, PhD
Vice President of Academic Affairs
Hennepin Technical College
Brooklyn Park, MN

Nyamwaya captures what should be a given for all leaders but unfortunately is not. This concept is such a fascinating read! Cultural Humility is what the world needs and hopefully Ms. Nyamwaya's words will strike a chord throughout the entire country. I particularly liked the Call to Learn. You are not only educated by the words so eloquently written but you are given the ability to put what you learn into practice. As stated in her book, Cultural Humility is "Just and Fair". Kudos to Ms. Nyamwaya for writing such a timely, thoughtful, and intelligent book for leaders, learners, and people from every walk of life. I definitely recommend it to every leader!

Pamela Percival
Senior Vice President
American Classic Agency
Jacksonville, Florida

Nyamwaya has masterfully illustrated the power of privilege and the distinction between wielding it recklessly versus using it to create positive impact. "Leading with Cultural Humility" is a must read for everyone who desires to transform a culture that was built on enslavement and genocide. Not only is this book packed with information, but also practical tools to aid an individual who is on the journey to becoming an ally.

Jonte' M. Robinson
Chief Diversity, Equity & Inclusion Officer
Sound Transit - Seattle, WA

So many people who were born and raised here (USA), many of whom have never experienced a prolonged stay in another culture, could benefit from the dose of cultural humility that is provided through your stories, teaching and observations. Your book will be helpful to hiring managers and coworkers, college instructors and classmates, social service leaders, and friends of New Americans, to newcomers who are observing and adjusting to an unfamiliar culture themselves, and to anyone who is curious about the interplay of dominant and non-dominant cultures. We are a blended nation of New Americans, Native Americans, individuals who came here willingly or whose ancestors came here seeking a better life, and those whose ancestors were forced here against their will. Our country is in need of healing. Our violent history and violent present, the systemic racism and discrimination that is woven into the fabric of our society requires a shift in hearts and minds. Your book teaches us to recognize the way we think about ourselves and others, how to shift our minds toward cultural humility and curiosity, and provides us with the potential to change the way we treat one another. Thank you for sharing these much-needed tools with us.

Brooke Anttila
Program Manager of Medical Career Advancement,
International Institute of Minnesota, MN

This book teaches one to focus on understanding others and asking beyond the bias given to them by society. It's important as a business owner and a human being to be aware of your biases and push to not let them cloud your judgment. Companies and people in power will never be able to succeed if they do not stop and ask their customers and employees what they can do to improve. I would recommend this book to people who struggle with seeing others' individuality but rather push groups of people together and assume they all have the same needs/wants. As a business owner myself, I am able to succeed when I ask my customers personal questions to understand why they need my services rather than just assume what they need and what they don't need because I've worked with someone in a similar situation.

Douglas Eze
CEO Largo Financial Services
Greenbelt, MD

Lyna captured my attention from all the questions we all think out loudly, silently or privately. She challenges the leader to remember that we all have biases and how we lead determines if people feel Seen, Heard and Valued. Lyna gracefully empowers you as a leader to keep steering the ship of your organization through the current times by doing the just right thing. This book emphasizes the importance of leading with humility and self-reflection and become aware that we positively or negatively create an impact. I recommend this book as a resource for anyone who serves people.

Caroline Mbithi-Dey
Holistic Health WealthPrenuer
Dallas, TX

Lyna has done an awesome job of connecting real life experiences through a cultural humility lens. For years, I have listened to and worked with Lyna on various leadership roles. In her book, Leading with Cultural Humility, Lyna excellently and skillfully challenges us to use our titles and positions to justly serve humanity and make the world a better place. For any leader who seeks to manage biases and make people feel seen, heard, and valued, this is a great book for you!

Jackline Ongwenyi MBA, RN, BSN
(Former Assistant Manager Maple Grove Hospital, MN 2019-2022)
Director of Nursing
Arise Homecare Services
Minneapolis, MN

Lyna Nyamwaya is one of my favorite nurses. Her history of overcoming every obstacle in her way and bringing as many people as possible along with her, is worthy of great admiration. Now she has added this book, "Leading with Cultural Humility" to her list of accomplishments. Though I had never heard the term Cultural Humility prior to reading Ms. Nyamwaya's book, it strikes a definite chord in my heart. We all must realize that none of us are knowledgeable of all cultures, because that would require mind-reading ability when meeting every person, we encounter. Nyamwaya's book definitely speaks to me and would do the same to you if you want to create cultures of belonging.

Leanne Meier, BSN, RN
Online Talk Show Host "Once a Nurse, Always a Nurse"
Founding Member of Nurses Transforming Healthcare
Minneapolis, MN

Empowering, informative, compelling! In her breakthrough book, Lyna gently and clearly guides the reader through concepts that can be intimidating to consider alone. With poise and compassion, Lyna shares about her personal experiences with racism and how she learned to understand this work was necessary. Weaved throughout the book are real-life examples, actionable insights, and opportunities for growth. Lyna connects all of it through a lens of greater humanity and the power we each have within to improve our world through cultural humility. If you consider yourself a leader who genuinely cares about your people, then this book is a must read.

Jennifer Anne Garcia
Career Coach, Founder, Writer
Best Resume Coach & LOVELeaf
Dallas, TX

This book is written from the heart, from personal experience. In a balanced way, Lyna makes a strong case for self-reflection regarding bias across cultures and a commitment to life-long learning of new ways to mitigate our own biases. A must have for any leader intentional about an indelible DEI&B footprint in their organization.

Edwin N. Bogonko, MD
Minnesota Medical Association, Board Chair
Chief Medical Officer, DiaspoCare
Minneapolis, MN

This is a great book for any leader because the cultural humility approach makes so much sense. It reminds us to ask our teams how they like to be appreciated rather than deciding for folks so we can decrease turnover, save millions of dollars in retention and grow our organizations. I strongly recommend this book to anyone, especially someone in a leadership role.

Anthony Stewart
President of American Classic Agency
CEO Stewart Financial Services
Lanham, MD

Lyna captures cultural humility as a strong strategic approach to leadership. As leaders, we do not run away from our biases. Instead, we acknowledge and manage them so we can be fair and fully embrace all the people we serve to create a positive and legacy impact. This is a great book for those who believe in true servant leadership.

Rose Oginga
Author, Unmasking Bullying In Schools
CEO Designed for Success Group
Tampa, Florida

For serious leaders only . . . Lyna Nyamwaya puts on an absolute clinic as it pertains to effectiveness and inclusivity in leadership. *Leading With Cultural Humility* is a well-researched, practical resource that addresses both the obvious and more obscure barriers to diversity, equity, inclusion, and belonging. This book is a must-read for true servant leaders who want to invoke meaningful change within their organizations.

Dr. Carl Stokes Jr.
Award-Winning Social Worker
President & CEO of Stokes Media
Buffalo, NY

Nyamwaya uses real life experiences to help us learn and unlearn our biases. This is very relevant in today's world where we have to co-exist as brothers and sisters.

Mukurima Muriuki, MA.
Founder, MBS Conflict Group
Long Beach, California

Gaining a deep understanding of bias with its many facets is critical to being able to recognize and change the dynamic for better outcomes. With tremendous insight and engaging examples from her own experience, Lyna provides important lessons and practical tools to become an effective and positive influencer for any endeavor.

Chris A. Stuart, MD
Chief Medical Officer/President (2015-2020)
Family Physician (2001-Present)
Northwest Family Clinics
Minneapolis, MN

With a lens of care and clarity, Nyamwaya expertly weaves America's contemporary social context with her tangible experience through masterful storytelling for an authentic and practical guide for awareness of the importance of cultural humility. The healthcare field is at the forefront of America's cultural crossroads, as all populations seek medical aide. This timely, and necessary, book offers a powerful testimony of the compassion and wisdom that our healthcare practitioners experience through consistent engagement in a multicultural reality. Nyamwaya offers a poignant and powerful reminder that the heart of healthy and sustaining leadership practices, aimed at inclusion and unity in our community, reside in cultural humility.

Thomas Malewitz, Ph.D.
Director, Ed.D.: Leadership Program
Spalding University

LEADING

with

CULTURAL HUMILITY

12 Inclusive Practices to Manage Biases, Promote Equity, and Cultivate Cultures of Belonging

LYNA NYAMWAYA

Copyright © 2022 by Bold Impact Group LLC

Cover design by Tri Widyatmaka
Editing by Jessica Sipos, PhD & Ann Maynard
Book Design by Mayfly Design
Author photograph by Jabari Holloman

For further information, including bulk orders of this book, please visit www.boldimpactgroup.com or send inquiries directly to lyna@boldimpactgroup.com.

1st edition, November 2022
ISBN: 979-8-9866878-0-3
Library of Congress Catalog Number: 2022921313
Printed in the United States of America

Many people have inspired the writing of this book.

To my grandmother, who had no formal education, professional training, or any standardized intelligence qualifier, yet was the realest and truest example of excellent inclusive leadership. You raised me to speak for the unheard and taught me that a simplest action of kindness can soften the hardest of hearts. I aim to practice kindness.

To the most brilliant and beautiful humans in the world, Kaylyn "KK", Makayla, Tanley and Tayden, may you always be kind and use your intelligence to stand up for justice because your Creator demands it. "I love you infinity" and I am proud that you are ours.

To every leader, present or future, who understands that leadership matters. May you strive to change unjust actions, honor good acts, and use your privilege for good. Cheers to your inclusive leadership journey.

Contents

CONTENTS

Why This Book?

It took a once-a-century crisis—the COVID-19 pandemic—to highlight police brutality against African Americans when we witnessed the murder of George Floyd in broad daylight.

It took this crisis to expose racial disparities in healthcare when we witnessed the death and unfair treatment of so many.

It took this crisis to recognize the nurses' excellent leadership skills in and out of crisis situations.

It took this crisis to appreciate teachers and see their value when parents had to take on the responsibility of instructing their own children.

It took this crisis to educate the world about systemic racism in America.

It has also taken this crisis for the Great Resignation to occur because people don't feel respected or valued.

In addressing these inequities, companies have spent billions of dollars since 2020 on the work of diversity, equity, inclusion, and belonging (DEIB) because they understand the benefits and want the rewards of inclusion. However, most leaders are frustrated because they have seen very few results, if any. Many leaders are now asking what else do we need to do to decrease disparities, promote inclusion, save money, and make people feel a sense of belonging? This question led me to write this book.

Twenty-five years ago, I had the privilege of coming to America as an international student. Throughout my 20-plus years of nursing as well as non-profit and education leadership and consulting, I have had many experiences and heard many stories of culture shock, biases, and cultural humility, both as a follower and leader. About 10 years ago, I founded a non-profit organization for immigrant and refugee healthcare professionals of African descent. These professionals found a safe space to share their stories of struggle and success. They mentioned the challenges of being "othered" and having to move across cities sometimes states, to seek the same services from places that made them feel valued. They shared how one day they would be experiencing immigrant privilege and the next day, xenophobia. After many years of sharing our experiences, we realized that we have many intersections of our diversity and had become members or employees of various equal opportunity institutions and organizations, but we didn't feel seen, heard, or respected. We also know of leaders who mentored and gave us a sense of belonging by reframing their approach. Instead of saying "I treat everyone how I like to be treated, they asked people how they would like to be treated. This takes away assumptions and focuses on meeting the needs of those you serve.

I wrote this book to offer you, as a leader, a different approach to making people feel safe, secure and supported. I offer you applicable practices to recognize and manage biases, recognize and use your power and privilege to do good, and become an open-minded, inclusive leader who creates excellent impact. We know that followers gravitate towards an inclusive leader before they buy into any vision. Students look forward to the instruction and guidance of a teacher who gives them a sense of belonging. Patients will not follow a regimen from a provider they feel is rude and condescending. People will leave companies with great pay because of bad leaders or stay at great companies with average pay because of inclusive leaders. In other words, leaders impact their followers positively or negatively. This book offers you an opportunity to become an effective, inclusive leader who not only saves millions of dollars by decreasing turnover and increasing retention but also builds a positive company reputation and lasting impactful relationships.

Through self-reflection, stories, studies, exercises, and activities, this book will challenge you to recognize some intentional or unintentional mistakes you can avoid in matters DEIB. I hope you will discover an approach and develop skills to navigate and engage in uncomfortable and challenging discussions to manage your biases, utilize your privilege to create a positive impact, improve communication, promote equity and inclusion, and cultivate cultures of belonging. These are cultures in any context where people, especially those from marginalized, underrepresented, disadvantaged, and minoritized groups, feel safe, secure, and supported. May this be an invaluable resource in your inclusive leadership journey.

Introduction

What Is This All About?

*We are in such sensitive times. I feel like I am walking on
eggshells.*
I am afraid of saying the wrong thing.
I am tired of being blamed for my privilege.
Not another diversity workshop!
Surely, we have done a gazillion cultural competency trainings.
We cannot save the world!
*Have we not put up enough signs to express our support for their
communities?*
Just tell me how much I should donate to keep them quiet.
*We have hired diverse teams into our organizations. What else
do they want?*
We cannot find any minority talent to fit our company.
We know they will keep using the race or gender or disability card.
Being Black is trending right now. Let them enjoy the season.
They should not be offended because I had good intentions.
I am aware that I have biases. What next?
How can I move from well-meaning to well-doing?
But how do I become more inclusive?

f you have said, heard, thought, or think of saying these statements, then this book is for you.

Throughout my professional career, I have heard many of my peers, colleagues, and leaders say that when it comes to the work of diversity, equity, inclusion and belonging (DEIB), they have read a lot of literature on creating awareness of biases and highlighting the benefits of inclusion. They have attended many workshops and trainings. However, they feel frustrated and are afraid of saying the wrong thing. They feel uncomfortable and unequipped to contribute, which makes them feel like they are walking on eggshells. I agree that nobody should feel overly tentative. I also agree that no one likes to feel guilty for having privilege, unearned or otherwise. However, as leaders, we have a responsibility to recognize and use our power and privilege, from our titles and positions, to create a positive impact. While we may not save the world, we can definitely improve the lives of the many people we interact with each day.

I believe that most humans are kind, compassionate, and want to do the right thing. I also believe most leaders recognize their responsibility to address the persistent racial tensions, centuries-old gender inequalities, and the hurtful discriminatory practices targeting race, gender, religion, age, class, nationality, sexual orientation, and disability that affect the marginalized, minoritized, underrepresented, disadvantaged, and underserved in our organizations.

While we have come a long way, the global uprising that erupted after the murder of George Floyd, a Black man, by a police officer, a White man, in Minneapolis, Minnesota, in May 2020, highlighted the ongoing racism and discriminatory practices entrenched in our systems. In the words of Martin Luther King Jr, "We must learn to live together as brothers and sisters or perish together as fools." We can all agree that the current demographic changes and technological advancements demand that we adapt and find solutions to our challenges, or we will continue to live in tension.

The good news is that DEIB work is an active process as natural and challenging to humans as any change we encounter. We just need a practical and applicable approach that works in any environment. This book aims to share that approach with you. But first, we must overcome some DEIB limiting beliefs.

Overcoming the DEIB Limiting Beliefs

We know that languages and cultures are always evolving. We also must evolve in our communication and interactions so we can cultivate cultures of belonging where people feel seen, heard, and valued. As a DEIB consultant, I have heard many leaders share several accepted reasons why DEIB is not a priority. These are some of the limiting beliefs why DEIB work hasn't worked:

- There is no budget for DEIB work at this time.
- We cannot find the right leaders in the minority pool to lead DEIB work.
- We have good intentions, so people need to stop being offended.
- We don't want to offend or lose our sponsors.
- We have always done it this way. Why change now?
- What if we invest in this DEIB project and it doesn't work?
- We are too busy with bigger fish to fry. DEIB work can wait.

One of the major and common themes I have noticed is that many leaders look at the DEIB work as a separate project, an accessory, not a main strategic vision in an organization or institution. What do I mean by "accessory?" Take the example of buying a cell phone, a necessary technological and communication device in modern society. When we set out to buy a cell phone, we have an option to buy accessories such as earbuds or screen protectors. We can buy the phone with or without them. We can use it without them because they are just complementary, at an extra cost. They are a nice thing to have because they make using our phones easier and more convenient. They are not necessary to the purpose and function of the phone, however. They are "extras."

When we approach DEIB work as an accessory, we think DEIB work is a nice "extra" option. We think, really, that it is "optional." That our institution and organization can survive without it. Perhaps it can, but it will not thrive. DEIB work is an integral part of organizational success and strategic planning. Why? Because DEIB work is *human* work, and any organization that has humans at its center will need to think about these concerns one way or another.

Unfortunately, too many organizations still consider DEIB work to be an add-on accessory to the organization where other strategic goals are the priority. They are afraid of losing sponsors, revenue, or doing the wrong thing. At the same time, studies show that the major reason for the Great Resignation during the COVID-19 pandemic was that most people were quitting because they did not feel appreciated or valued. We can no longer assume that we are doing enough with and for the people in our organizations. We must intentionally invest time and resources to build cultures of belonging. Fortunately, there is an approach to overcoming limiting beliefs and building cultures of belonging.

Cultural Humility: A Different Approach to DEIB

I wrote this book to offer leaders a different approach to diversity, equity, inclusion and belonging. How is it different? First of all, I offer my insights from my position as a woman of the global majority with many intersections of diversity. I am an educator, a registered nurse leader, a non-profit president, and an immigrant to the United States. I realize that humans have different perceptions and perspectives depending on our different upbringings, backgrounds, and cultures. That is not necessarily "good" or "bad." We are just different. We just need to acknowledge our differences and harness the strength in our diversity so we can realize positive outcomes.

A few years ago, my mentor, Dr. RS, introduced me to the notion of cultural humility. Cultural humility challenges us to identify and manage biases, recognize and utilize our power and privilege to create a positive impact, and stay open to learning. In this book, we explore the cultural humility approach and inclusive practices to promote equity and inclusion and build cultures of belonging in any classroom, breakroom, boardroom, breakout room, lunchroom, restroom, or any other room.

As leaders, we must recognize our duty to do the work to make people feel seen, heard, and valued. This has outcomes beyond how people feel; it promotes retention, decreases turnover, increases innovation, productivity, and employee engagement, saves millions of dollars by avoiding preventable lawsuits, and cultivates cultures of belonging. Unless we make inclusive leadership a priority, we will lose great people, have difficulty retaining them, and tarnish our reputations because we have not identified and addressed the needs of those we serve.

The solution is utilizing the cultural humility approach to self-reflect on our beliefs and backgrounds, recognizing our power and privilege as well as our limitations when it comes to knowing and serving others, then learning to listen and focus on those we serve so we can effectively lead them.

Being Inclusive is Just . . . and Just Economical

Studies show that being inclusive improves communication, which promotes engagement and builds lasting relationships. It saves money by decreasing employee turnover, promoting retention, increasing innovation and productivity, and enhancing company reputation. In education, inclusion increases student and teacher motivation, performance, and achievement. Being inclusive and equitable gives those we serve and interact with a sense of belonging.

Several studies show workers have left jobs due to toxic work culture, and not feeling respected or valued. Further studies show that unmanaged biases, even from well-intentioned leaders, negatively affect those we serve. Some examples of unmanaged biases in toxic environments include:

- Discrimination
- Gossip
- Double standards
- Unfairness
- Microaggressions
- Racial trauma
- Inappropriate behaviors

I could go on and on about the benefits of inclusion, but fundamentally, inclusion is important because it is the right and just thing to do. Considering such times as these, where some people feel oppressed and demand to be liberated while others feel sensitive to and inconvenienced by these demands, I wrote this book for leaders who are not afraid of doing the right thing. It is for leaders who want to improve communication and increase engagement. It's for leaders who want to serve clients and leave them feeling seen, heard, and valued. It is also for pragmatic leaders who want to save millions on preventable lawsuits. Mostly, I wrote this book for leaders who want to create a lasting positive impact and create reputable organizations that give the marginalized, minoritized, underrepresented, disadvantaged, and underserved a sense of belonging. Effective leaders lead with kindness, curiosity, courage, compassion, and a commitment to listening with empathy to understand. They begin, serve, and end with equity and inclusion.

Through self-reflection, stories, statements, and exercises, this book will challenge you to recognize and manage your biases, develop skills to navigate challenging times, and engage in uncomfortable often challenging discussions to build cultures of belonging. It is through interpersonal strategy that we build lasting relationships and legacy leadership. My hope is that by reading this book, you will discover an applicable approach to improve communication, activate your power and privilege into allyship, promote equity and inclusion, and create cultures, in any context, where everyone feels seen, heard, and valued.

I hope reading this book inspires you to become more effective and inclusive in your leadership. Let us remember to extend grace to ourselves when we make a mistake and remain authentic as we discover new knowledge and understanding. By the same token, let us extend grace to others as they learn, as well. Together, we will create a ripple effect to cultivate cultures of belonging where people feel safe, secure, and supported. Let's move beyond good intentions and create excellent impact.

From Culture Shock to Cultural Humility

Do not insult those you are trying to impact. —African Proverb

My American Culture Shock Story

Once my host picked me up and we left Chicago's O'Hare airport, it was literally a cold welcome in August of 1997. I didn't know I needed to pack or dress warmly because we didn't discuss the weather. Many days following, I was in sundresses when I should have been in warm pants. Dressing in layers, two pairs of pants would have been laughable or labeled madness in Kenya. I was once fooled by the bright fall sunshine, so I put on a light African dress. It was only a matter of minutes until I could not feel my ears because my fingers, nose, and toes were nearly frozen. On our way home from the airport the day I arrived, we stopped at Arby's to get something to eat. I could not recognize many items on the menu. All I really wanted was chicken and chips. My American cousins, Brian and Travis, quickly corrected me that I should ask for chicken and fries. I also wanted "tomato sauce" and a soda. "Cousin Lyna, you need ketchup and pop. Tomato sauce is for cooking!"

Weeks later, I realized that ordering food at the drive-through was harder than sitting inside the restaurant because not only did I struggle to find what I wanted to order on the screen, they could not understand what I was saying through the intercom. I came to the USA speaking English with a Kenyan-British accent, yet I was "pardon me'ed" every other word. At the drive-thru, I was often misunderstood and ended up with the wrong food, sometimes even something I couldn't eat, so I wound up hungry. This was frustrating and demoralizing.

Soon I was in class at my new college: English 101. In Kenya, I had been writing compositions since the fourth grade. But guess what? I had to learn to spell simple words and eliminate letters without remorse. For example, "colour" no longer had a "u." The past tenses of learn and dream weren't "learnt" or "dreamt." Can you imagine saying "schedule" like "school" when I had been saying "shed-yule" all my life? It felt like I had to deliberately speak "wrong," but here, I was the "wrong" one! My instructor reminded me that as a writer, I must always mind my audience and remember that language is not just about being technically "correct" (according to my standards!) but is for communication, however best my readers and listeners can understand me. I started to speak slowly, repeat myself, and clarify if I had to make sure my listener got the message. As a multilingual speaker—English is my third language after Ekegusii and Kiswahili—I know that language is not a measure of intelligence but a form of communication. I believe if we would be instructed and tested in our native languages, we would all be geniuses. Perhaps it seems I am taking longer to speak or get my message across. This may be accurate because I think in my mother tongue, Ekegusii, before mentally translating to English to communicate my thoughts to the people around me here in the United States.

I also remember when I got lost on campus for hours and ended up missing the whole class. Many new students get lost on campus. When you are lost, everyone gives directions using cardinal directions. (At least, this is the case in the Midwest!) They will say, "Go north, then turn right." They will describe the location of your room as being on the east side of the building. So, since no one told me to bring a small pocket compass, I just started early because I knew I would get lost. Budget at least 1-2 hours of "getting-lost" time! The good news is eventually you will find your room or the class you are looking for. The bad news, class will be over.

Then I would have to get lost on my way home. Every road or street has a name. Some streets are one way. Once on one, it might be a while before getting off. Oh, by the way, don't get lost on the highway! When I finally made it to class, I realized that to understand the American accent, I had to really listen because American English has a very different accent compared to British English or Kenyan English.

From Culture Shock to Cultural Humility

A few years ago, I met my mentor for lunch. I was excited to share with her observations my grandmother, Baba, expressed while visiting me for the first time in the United States. Baba and I were at church when she saw a little girl with bits of metal over her teeth. Baba was shocked and had many questions. First, she asked if the child was all right. She then wondered why the girl's mother would "do that to her baby." She was even more concerned when she learned that kids sleep and eat with this metal on their teeth. She thought it seemed cruel and painful. To her, it seemed torturous that a child would have their teeth pulled for months, or even years, for the sake of culture. Interestingly, Baba forgot that she was missing her two bottom front teeth, which had been removed many years before in a traditional practice as standard in Kenya as orthodontic braces are in America. Yet she believed the braces in a little American girl's mouth were abnormal and tortur-

11

ous. It would be one of many culture shocks Baba experienced on her trip. She saw her own cultural practices as unremarkable and even superior to the American customs she was observing.

My mentor smiled at my story and then shared a similar experience. When she first saw pictures of little Maasai girls with beads around their necks and ornaments hanging from their earlobes, she, like Baba, was shocked. Like Baba, she said, "To be honest, it seemed painful." The Maasai, a Kenyan tribe, have several cultural practices that appear painful or inexplicable to people not from their communities.

Cultural biases happen when we perceive other cultures as bad, sad, painful, less than, or not good enough compared to our own. We can also have cultural biases that elevate another culture as superior to our own. Left unmanaged, our biases can harm others. This is where our work begins. Biases emerge from ethnocentrism, which is the interpretation and judgment of others by standards inherent to one's own culture. It is a problem because we humans struggle with epistemic plurality, that is, the ability to hold more than one viewpoint simultaneously and see the value in multiple views of the world. That day, over lunch, my mentor introduced me to cultural humility, a concept coined in 1998 by two doctors, Melanie Tervalon and Jann Murray-Garcia. It is a three-part framework that includes self-reflection, recognizing power imbalances, and being open to the continuous process of learning. The two physicians, wanting to improve racial relations in their community after the police savagely beat Rodney King, created a space where their community members could listen and learn about each other's culture. They asked each person to research their origin and history. They then invited them to present their findings to the group.

At the end of their study, the two doctors concluded that the commonly taught method of "cultural competence" is limited in that it provides information about groups from only one perspective. They also realized that it is impossible to be competent in a culture, as culture is ever-changing and highly contested even within a shared culture group. They were amazed at how many subcultures are unknown and unrecognized and concluded that it is crucial to reflect on our own cultures and recognize how they shape and affect how we see those with whom we interact or serve. Tervalon and Murray-Garcia thus developed the concept of cultural humility that allows people to see others as unique individuals with their own cultural backgrounds and experiences.

Years later, the National Institutes of Health (NIH) defined cultural humility as "a lifelong process of self-reflection and self-critique whereby the individual not only learns about another's culture, but one starts with an examination of her/his own beliefs and cultural identities." Cultural humility challenges us not to focus on our knowledge and expertise but on the limitations of that knowledge so we can ask questions and listen more to learn from each unique person we serve.

What About "Cultural Competence?"

As a registered nurse, my education and professional training demanded that I become "culturally competent." In preparation for clinical practice, taking care of patients in a healthcare setting, we had to read about their backgrounds and cultural beliefs based on their race, country of origin, or ethnicity and how traits may ostensibly affect their care. It was during this time that I realized cultural competence offers information about a group or population from a single perspective, a Western perspective, which tends to scientifically order and label the world into categories and traits. While beneficial in some ways, such as the scientific method that has yielded great discoveries, it is a problematic way to approach the complexity of humanity. Some of our texts explained, for instance, that most Asian patients prefer warm water; African-American patients view disease and death as a punishment from their Creator, God; Latino patients exaggerate expressions of pain, and Native American patients are mostly non-compliant in following their practitioner-ordered regimen and rely more on healers.

While cultural "competence" can only go so far as a form of basic, superficial, generalized knowledge, I argue that true competence is not possible. Culture is not something "mastered." Anthropologists, scholars of culture, tend to understand the complexities and nuances of culture and would hesitate to declare themselves culturally "competent." Indeed, culture is something "practiced." The late Dr. Paul Farmer, a renowned medical anthropologist, was fluent in French and Haitian Creole and had a deep knowledge of the culture, economics, politics, and history of Haiti, where he worked and lived for 35 years. Still, he stated he was never "competent" in Haitian culture. Whenever someone is allegedly talking about "culture" and they are doing it in a manner that is rigidly bounded or homogenous—essentializing—or used to deny people equity, they are really talking about the social construction of a culture, such as race, ability, or gender, and so on. This generalization hurts more than it helps.

The cultural competence approach "essentializes" humans to their most basic, group-associated traits and values, ones that may not apply to that individual before us. As nurses, we are taught a list of "cultural characteristics" that are supposed to help health care workers take care of their diverse patients. How can someone ever be "competent" in a culture where they can't speak the language and have zero knowledge about the social, cultural, economic, political, or historical context that shapes that culture? When leaders focus only on cultural competence, they miss opportunities to ask questions with curiosity, listen with empathy, and be open to learning about their team members' cultures and learning styles. Cultural competence leads us to think we can "know" another culture; we believe culture is something to "master." This can lead to hubris and even misguided attempts to "teach" others about their own culture or even argue when they try to teach us. Furthermore, culture is not static or entirely agreed upon, even by members of the same culture. Needless to say, after several years of practice, my colleagues and I have identified many limitations of cultural competence—and those limitations can lead to unintended negative consequences.

How is Cultural Humility Different?

Nurse Mora had thoroughly read the patient's chart to gain insight into his needs and how his cultural practices might affect his care. And, citing cultural competence, she surmised that since her patient was from a certain town in Minnesota and belonged to a particular race, he must be Lutheran. This is because most people from that city are Lutheran. In trying to support the patient and let the daughter spend time with her father, Nurse Mora offered to call chaplaincy services. She went ahead and paged the chaplain line and requested a Lutheran minister. A few moments later, the chaplain arrived, and she showed him to the patient's room. The patient's daughter, who had been holding her father's hand while waiting, was excited to see the two return so promptly. However, she was unsure why a Lutheran minister was standing at her father's bedside. The daughter looked disappointed as she told Nurse Mora and the chaplain that her father didn't need a Lutheran minister. Instead, he needed a rabbi. The nurse apologized profusely to her patient, the daughter, and the chaplain. The chaplain left the room to page for a rabbi. As Nurse Mora tearfully recounted the story to our team, we all realized that good intent doesn't equal good impact. If only she had stopped to ask the patient's daughter what her father's preference was, she could have avoided the disappointment and saved time and resources. There would have been a happy family whose needs were met by a remarkable nurse. Using a cultural humility approach, Nurse Mora would not have made a generalized assumption about the patient's religion. All it would have taken was asking one more question to determine the individual patient's preference.

Cultural humility addresses the limitations of cultural competence by challenging people to reflect on their origins, how that origin affects actions and decisions, and recognize how power and privilege may affect others. It reminds us to stay open to learning. We can apply cultural humility practices in any educational, healthcare, sports, criminal justice, faith community, correctional or law enforcement setting to promote inclusion. Recognizing demographic changes and technology advancements that bring people from all over the world together in collaboration (and conflict), leaders need skills to develop the capacity for deep reflection to acknowledge their biases and listen better with empathy to see and hear their teams or clients.

Cultural humility means being upfront about the reality that our understanding of other people's cultures is always limited. We need to be open to learning from other people about their culture, seeing the differences as neither "good" nor "bad" but just different. Leading with cultural humility challenges us to reflect on what we know about our own cultures of origin as well as consider what we do not yet know or understand about other people's cultures so we can listen with empathy and, in return, improve communication and promote inclusion and retention. A cultural humility approach gives us an opportunity to ask more questions, engage in conversation, and learn more about people to see and understand them first as the unique individuals they are. We can always be in a position to LEARN.

Embracing cultural humility as a practice, leaders can offer services that elevate the humanity and dignity of everyone in-

Listen to understand, not to reply.

Evaluate our feelings before we respond.

Need to stay open to learning.

LEARN

Respond with empathy. Avoid the savior mentality.

Ask with curiosity to learn. Do not assume.

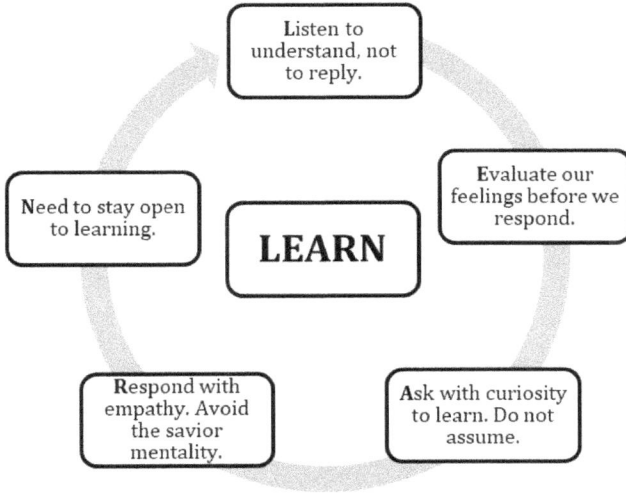

volved and create a positive and bold impact in the world. Leaders have a moral duty to mitigate biases. To manage biases, cultural humility challenges us to reflect on our own cultures and backgrounds, recognize what we know and may not know about those we are leading or serving, acknowledge and activate our power and privilege into allyship, and stay open to learning more deeply about ourselves and those we interact with.

All leaders must assess their interactions and relationships to determine whether their biases lead them to deny or extend opportunities. Acknowledging biases creates opportunities to assist those who may be disadvantaged. We share the responsibility to create cultures of belonging and make our world more inclusive.

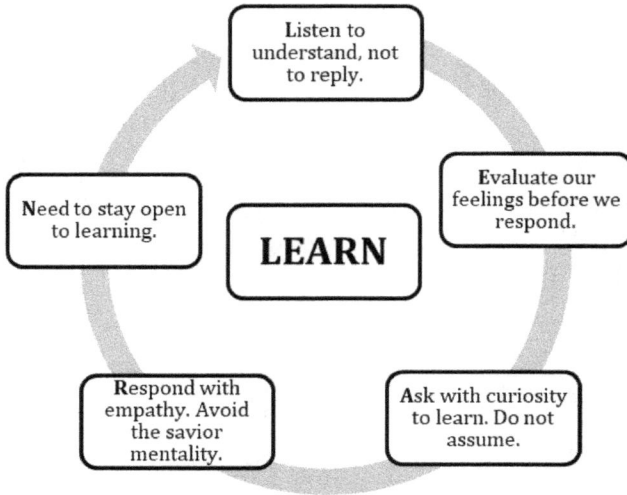

TAKEAWAYS

- We all have cultural biases. When unmanaged, they harm others.
- Cultural competence views people from a group's perspective, while cultural humility views people as individuals with unique needs.

CALL TO LEARN

- Describe one of your culture shock experiences.
- Identify an approach to advance your DEIB leadership journey.

MISTAKE #1

I do not have biases.

1

Biases Are Human

*In the end anti-black (sic), anti-female, and all forms of discrimination are
equivalent to the same thing: anti-humanism.* —Shirley Chisholm

What are Biases?

We often think of biases as things that exist somewhere *out there*. Other people have biases, not us. We know they are harmful or hurtful. We know they exist. It is just that they exist *out there*, far away from us. We think we are the ones who are bias-free, colorblind, equal opportunity, fair. Do you know why we think this way?

The thought of having biases makes us uncomfortable. We don't like to talk about things that make us uncomfortable. We were taught that biases are bad, and we don't want to be seen as racist or homophobic or discriminatory. We don't even like to think about such things, much less admit they could be true about us. We worry they might expose realities about our thoughts or feelings that we are not willing or ready to address. We do not know how to. Perhaps we prefer not to acknowledge such uncomfortable truths—and sometimes, we may not even be aware of them. If we are leaders, we may even fear appearing unsure because we are supposed to be experts or more knowledgeable than everyone else. It is easier to deflect the discussion altogether, lest someone sees and judges that weakness. Yes, it is so much easier to talk about the weather and work deadlines.

Effective leaders must address both the comfortable and the uncomfortable stuff. We cannot shy away from these essential conversations. We must be willing to face the uncomfortable, to bring it into the light—first for ourselves and then for those we lead.

Recognize Our Biases

About 25 years ago, I had the privilege of traveling from Nairobi, Kenya, to America for further studies. It was the first flight I had ever taken, over 24 hours of travel time, and I was young, curious, and scared.

After a connection in London and another layover in Boston, I safely landed in Chicago, Illinois. I stepped off the jetway and proceeded to baggage claim while tightly clutching my backpack, which I wore on my chest because I had been warned that someone might slip drugs into my bag or steal my only belongings. I had to be on the lookout. So, you can imagine my shock when I realized that everyone else was minding their business and paying no attention to me. What surprised me more was how strangers smiled at me—it's a gesture we don't do to strangers where I grew up. Smile at our friends and family or familiar faces, of course! But to people we don't know? It was my first taste of culture shock, and it zapped my fear into curiosity. That experience developed my love for traveling and increased my curiosity to see the world.

Since then, I have become an expert traveler. I fly all over the world to educate and inspire other leaders, as I believe sharing knowledge is the most effortless way to change lives. I remember my last trip before the COVID-19 pandemic put a halt to travel in 2020. I was heading to an educator's conference in Dallas, Texas. I got up early and called an Uber to take me to the airport in Minneapolis. The ride was a pleasant one, and my driver and I exchanged a bit of small talk. When we arrived, I thanked the driver for getting me to the airport safely in time for my flight.

I called my husband from my gate to let him know I had checked in and made sure the kids had gotten up in time for school. As the boarding process began, I noticed some very happy-looking flight attendants who seemed remarkably bright-eyed for how early it was. As I stepped from the jetway to the plane, the pilot stood at the door and cheerfully greeted me, "Good morning! Welcome aboard and enjoy your flight!" The flight attendants were all smiles and seemed to enjoy their job. Considering I had hardly slept the night before, I couldn't wait to settle in my seat, so I could snooze some. As soon as I secured my safety belt and closed my eyes, I fell asleep.

I was woken up by an overhead announcement declaring that we had arrived at our destination. The flight crew remained happy and professional as they wished their departing passengers a great day. I arrived at my hotel after a short ride from the airport. I was a bit early, and my room wasn't ready yet, so I went to one of the hotel restaurants to grab breakfast. At the entrance, I was greeted and shown to my seat by a friendly and professional server who politely asked, "Ma'am, what would you like to drink?" They returned with what I wanted: a tall glass of refreshing and tasty fresh orange juice. Just what I needed to start my day. The restaurant was crowded and lively. Next to me sat a married couple who seemed to be enjoying their meal. They turned to me, smiled, and in unison, they said, "Good morning!" I smiled and wished them the same.

As soon as I finished eating, I checked into my room, changed into comfortable clothes, then headed to the conference room. As expected, the conference room was set up well, with good lighting. Attendees filled the room, and I was just in time as the speakers walked onto the stage. The event schedule indicated that a panel of top leaders from great institutions would start the day by discussing inclusive best practices that combat biases, improve communication, and create a culture of belonging in educational environments.

Now, thinking about my story, reflect on these questions:

- When I mentioned my Uber driver, who did you picture in your mind?
- Did you picture a male or female or transgender person?
- What was the Uber driver's ethnicity?
- What about the flight attendants? Were they male? Female? People of the global majority or the global minority?
- What about the pilot? Was the pilot male or female or transgender? People of the global majority or the global minority?
- What about the hotel staff at the restaurant? Who did you see? Were they differently abled? Were they male, female, or transgender? What was their ethnicity? Did their religion cross your mind?
- What about the married couple? Did you envision them as a male and female, male and male, female and female, or transgender couple?
- What about the panelists? Were they all male, female, transgender? People of the global majority or the global minority? What about their age? Were they younger or older? Did they have any physical disabilities or visible or invisible identifiers?

What about your responses surprised you? Could you see how your biases came into play? This exercise helps uncover our unconscious biases. We all have them. They are there, regardless of our intentions. The answers to my questions do not need to be shared with anyone. What matters is *we* are aware of our own unconscious biases.

We begin with awareness to recognize the problem itself, but it is only a start. Reflecting on biases and their origin is an essential practice, especially for people in leadership roles. When left unmanaged, unaddressed, or ignored, our biases can harm others in very real ways. Unconscious biases affect hiring, firing, student admissions, court convictions, job promotions, productivity, performance, mental health, and so many other aspects of our lives. They can limit opportunities, lead to wrongful accusations, inaccurate assessments, unfair treatment, and poor judgment. Biases also uphold and sustain faulty assumptions and stereotypes about certain persons or groups of people.

Leaders, especially those of us in human services industries, have a duty to recognize these biases and their effect on the decisions we make and the actions we take. Unconscious biases are also known as *implicit biases*. Psychologists describe unconscious biases as social stereotypes or prejudices that we form unaware about groups of people. Further, they define unconscious bias as prejudice or unsupported judgments in favor of or against one thing, person, or group compared to another in a way that is usually considered unfair or unjust. We all have biases. Even those of us who were raised to treat everyone with respect. Even those of us who are not racist. Even those of us who have great intentions coming from a good place. We all have biases.

Different Kinds of Biases

There are many kinds of implicit biases that influence and affect our leadership decisions. Below is a list of the most common, but it is by no means exhaustive. When unmanaged, even from well-intentioned persons, biases cause harm.

Affinity Biases

Maybe you have heard of the old saying "kind notices kind." We are attracted to those like us in race, age, sexuality, religion, or education. That means we favor those with whom we share the same background. Affinity biases can be especially impactful when hiring or admitting candidates. It can also favor some while hurting others. Ask yourself why you select or deselect a candidate. How might you extend opportunities to all?

Confirmation Biases

When we look for information that aligns with our already-formed perceptions, that's confirmation bias. For example, a teacher assumes students from a poor or low-income environment lack parental support and have no time to study. That teacher doesn't expect those students to excel—or expects them to fail—and that belief influences their grading. Another example is when an interviewer who offered me a job said, "I like Africans because they are hard workers. I don't like African Americans because they are lazy." There are so many things wrong with such stereotypical perceptions. Ask whether you may be inaccurately assuming and negatively grading or denying people opportunities.

Conformity Biases

I see a lot of conformity bias at play in social media groups such as Facebook or LinkedIn discussions. Our decisions are swayed or influenced by the views of others in the majority. Conformity bias is also known as "groupthink" because it is common in groups. We tend to act in a certain way because the majority of our team act that way. Before you allow yourself to be swayed by others' comments, examine your feelings and biases. Ask yourself: How well do I understand this issue? Is my decision or action influenced by others?

Gender Biases

When Margaret Thatcher became the prime minister of England and was asked to select her team, she intentionally chose men only. When offered an opportunity to select women, she declined and explained that she believed men make better leaders. Her assumption that one gender is better at a job or role than the other is a gender bias. We also see gender bias underpinning unequal pay practices, where men are paid more than women just because of their gender. Throughout my career, I have witnessed gender inequalities in the nursing industry. I have seen colleagues, both male and female, not question decisions by male doctors while they disrespect and question female doctors. I have seen and heard of managers who promote male nurses and give them shifts of preferences while passing up female nurses who, in fact, had more seniority and were more deserving than their male colleagues. Ask whether we believe certain genders are better suited to certain roles or tasks.

LEADING WITH CULTURAL HUMILITY

The Halo/Horn Effect

Humans have a tendency to see a person or group as superior after learning something impressive about them or their achievements. We also do the opposite: we see a person as inferior when we learn something negative or unfavorable about them. For example, when college leaders learn that a student candidate was at the top of their class and their parent is a doctor or professor, then they assume that that student is smart or automatically qualifies. On the other hand, when teachers learn that a student lives in poverty or comes from a poor background, they assume the student may not be smart enough and may likely fail. The Halo/Horn effect can impact decisions on admissions, hiring, and assignments. Therefore, ask yourself: Are my assessments or decisions partial or impartial?

Name Biases

The tendency to judge a person negatively based on their name or preconceived opinions about their background is called name bias. President Barack Hussein Obama is a particularly notable example. He was called un-American because of his "foreign-sounding" name, and his birth certificate was questioned by his political opponents. He was even associated with Muslim terrorists because of his middle name, and some feared him as a threat to America because of his name and presumed background. Name bias comes into play when hiring or admitting candidates by reviewing resumes or transcripts. Ask yourself: Am I judging others by their skill, qualifications, and experiences, or is my thinking influenced by my preconceived opinions about their names and background?

Weight and Body Size Bias

When we judge people negatively based on their body size or appearance, we are engaging in weight bias or size prejudice (size-ism). In some cultures, larger body types are seen as less favorable, while others view smaller body types as weak or sick. A few years ago, I flew to Kenya for my father's funeral. When checking in at the airport, the airline agent holding our family passports looked at the open passport in front of her and then studied my youngest baby in my husband's arms. "Are you sure that the child is 15 months old?" she asked. My first thought was to ask her what the passport said, but then I wondered, *if this agent doesn't believe the federal government, how do I expect her to believe me?* I politely said yes. As much as I wanted to educate her on her sizeism, I was exhausted and grieving. I wondered if her reaction would have been the same if my daughter had a smaller body size. Ask yourself: What assumptions do I make about a person, based on their weight, regarding their character, health status, or lifestyle?

Beauty Biases

When we judge people as more competent or qualified based solely on their attractive appearance, we're being swayed by beauty bias, also known as attribute bias. Based on societal standards or norms, we tend to think that attractive people are better or perform better at their job than those less attractive. This attractiveness scale typically views smaller-sized bodies of European descent as the norm, a bias in and of itself. Studies show that less attractive people struggle more to get a job compared to more attractive people. Beauty bias is also seen when leaders overlook the mistakes of those with a more attractive appearance and magnify those from the less attractive. Or those leaders who amplify the accomplishments of the more attractive people and overlook those of the less attractive people. Ask yourself: What assumptions do I make about people I consider attractive or unattractive?

Language Biases

We judge people based on how they sound and tend to relate to or like those who sound like us. We presume that those with a foreign or unfamiliar accent may not hear, understand, or communicate well enough to perform a job or role. Sometimes, some deselect or fail candidates because they have an accent with the presumption that they may not understand the exam requirements or job assignments. We make other assumptions too. For example, some people tend to raise their voices or automatically speak slowly when they realize I have an accent. Some automatically ask, "Where are you from?" Others say, "For someone from Africa, you speak really good English," and inquire about when or where I learned it. Ask yourself: What assumptions do I make when I hear someone speak with an unfamiliar accent? Do I view some accents more positively than others?

We Cannot Solve a Problem We Don't See

The biases described above are just a handful of the implicit (or overt) biases that may be influencing leadership decisions. Our beliefs developed from our societal or familial upbringing, beliefs, background, or cultures. While they may feel "true" to us, they require honest examination. When unmanaged, even from well-intentioned persons, biases cause harm.

Many leaders have asked me how they can manage biases to become more inclusive and create a sense of belonging. My answer is always the same: *You cannot solve a problem you don't see, and you cannot give what you don't have.* That's why managing our biases begins with self-evaluation and self-reflection. Self-evaluation allows you to understand what you know, where you are and where you want to be. Self-reflection helps you to recognize how your behaviors, perceptions, or responses are molded or affected by your backgrounds, beliefs, upbringing, and cultures. It allows you to know and tune in with your emotions so you can be honest with yourself about yourself and address your inner critic. Then we must recognize our power and privilege as it relates to and might affect those we serve or otherwise interact with. Doing right means applying the right action after recognizing who you are, why you feel certain emotions, and how your power and privilege affect those you interact with and serve.

When we understand ourselves and why we feel or act the way we do, we can understand others better, too. Understanding others builds relationships, improves communication, establishes boundaries, and acknowledges mistakes. When we are aware of our and others' emotions and know how to relate and communicate with them, we lead effectively. As leaders, we have a responsibility to acknowledge and adapt to these demographic changes and technological advancements. It starts by acknowledging our biases, both positive and negative, and recognizing our power and privilege to implement inclusive practices. Cultural humility creates a space for us to acknowledge our beliefs, admit the limitations of that knowledge, and focus on those we serve with empathy and curiosity. It means we do not assume control by treating eah person how we would like to be treated. Rather, ask each individual how they would like to be treated and then pay attention to the details so you can meet that unique human's needs. That is how you manage biases and build cultures of belonging.

Managing Biases is Not a One-Time Fix

After years of careful listening and research, I realized there is no one-size-fits-all solution when it comes to managing biases in matters of inclusion and belonging. Managing biases is not a project to be completed but a lifelong process that requires constant reflection on our backgrounds, beliefs, and cultures, management of our ideas and thoughts, and intentional action and decisions that utilize power and privilege to create a positive impact. It demands a willingness to take risks and make mistakes but own the responsibility to correct behavior or right wrongs.

Mistakes are inevitable. What was appropriate many years ago may be seen as inappropriate today. Words or language that did not seem to bother anyone a few years ago may be hurtful and offensive today. The way we thought of certain people long ago may be very different once you learn all history and hear their stories. The demographic makeup of our grade schools may be very different from the classrooms in our professional training or places of work. Current technological advancement has completely altered the way we read or socialize, process information, even prioritize current events, but those technologies, such as AI, are themselves embedded in structural racism.

These observations indicate that as culture, language, demographics, and technology evolve, our approach to diversity, equity, and inclusion must also evolve. A cultural humility lens allows you to view everyone as a human who deserves respect.

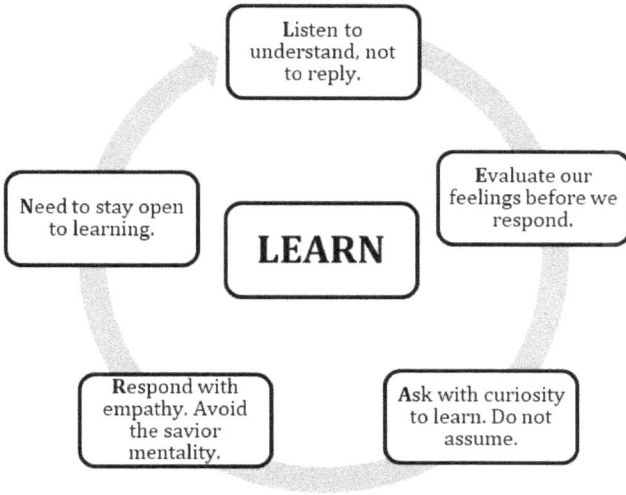

TAKEAWAYS

- We all have biases, and there are different types of biases.
- Managing biases is not a project to be completed or a problem to be fixed. It is a life-long process.

CALL TO LEARN

- Intentionally practice mitigating biases in all your interactions.
- Instead of treating people how you like to be treated, start asking people how they would like to be treated.

MISTAKE #2

---

*I do not have privilege;
I have worked hard for
what I have.*

2

Use Your Power and Privilege to Serve Humanity

No one is born hating another person because of the colour of his skin, or his background or his religion. People learn to hate, and if they can learn to hate, they can be taught to love, for love comes more naturally to the human heart than its opposite. —Nelson Mandela

Power and Privilege

"I am because you are" is the African philosophy of *ubuntu* which shows the nature of community and shared humanity. I am who and what I am because you are also. In this concept, humanity is seen and accorded the highest value and respect. Being human is powerful. It is a shared value and connectedness with other humans. However, reflecting on the historical background of the United States, power and privilege determine and affect human value.

Power is the capacity to direct or influence how others behave or the course of events. Ultimate power is that over life and death, both one's own and that of others. Most leaders have power and privilege through authority associated with an office, title, position, education, gender, or wealth.

Privilege, on the other hand, is "a special right, earned or unearned advantage, or immunity granted or available only to a particular person or group." In antiracism scholarship, privilege is defined as the *lack of barriers or obstacles* one has in life. To identify and determine the effects of privilege, it is necessary to notice that one particular person or group has special rights while other persons or groups may not. By definition, for one group to be dominant in power or authority means there is a non-dominant group. Privilege can be both an earned or unearned advantage; one can achieve a position of privilege or be born into it. Having privilege is not the same as having power, though they can certainly overlap. Privilege is not about what one has. It is about the obstacles or barriers that one has not had to overcome.

We have all heard stories highlighting age-old discriminatory practices that stem from abusing these advantages. These practices harm various groups by race, age, gender, sexual orientation, language, nationality, class, or education. There is no end to stories of harmful leaders who abuse both their power and privilege.

When We Stop Being Human, We Dehumanize People

One of the first stories I heard of such leaders was when Baba told me about a powerful but very despotic leader. This leader ordered his soldiers to gather all the disabled people from every village and town because he had a "special place" for them. He explained that since they were not working or contributing to the country's economy, he had found a place where they would benefit the country's economy. The soldiers gathered all the disabled people: the blind, deaf, lame, dumb, and anyone with a physical disability. There were many tears as families said goodbye to their loved ones, but no one dared question where they were be-

ing taken. If anyone resisted, they were shot dead or severely punished. The soldiers loaded the disabled people in big lorries (trucks) and drove away to the new "special place." The silence was loud as everyone watched. The soldiers drove and drove up to the biggest lake in the region, Lake Victoria (originally known as Nam Lolwe by the Luo people of Kenya). They stopped by the lake and dumped the people into the lake. Many of the people in the trucks couldn't see or hear or speak. Most of them couldn't swim. The soldiers kept watch to make sure no one escaped, waiting until each of their captives had drowned. It sounds unbelievable, like a dystopian novel, but the story is true. This leader used his position, the power bestowed on him by his title and authority, to destroy people. It is the story of the actions of Idi Amin, the former president of Uganda.

When we chose to abuse our power and privilege, we stop being human and dehumanize others.

On the other hand, I have benefited from privilege on many occasions. When I was new in America and looking for work as an international student, I signed on with an employment agency, also known as a temp agency. Here you would apply for a job and hope to get one. If they got you a job, they didn't give you employment benefits. However, you got paid weekly. This was heaven for an international student who had little time to learn about the importance of benefits. My time was better used to learning how to drive so I didn't have to ask for rides to school or work.

One day, there were five of us who had applied for a single job opening at a nursing home. I felt and knew I was qualified for the role, but I wasn't optimistic about my chances of getting the job. I didn't have as much experience as the other applicants, plus I didn't sound like them. I predicted the interviewer would ask me where I was from as soon as she heard my accent and then give me her regrets. However, during the interview, the woman told me she was happy with my qualifications and that she "preferred Africans anyway because they are hard workers." Looking back, I now see her own set of cultural stereotypes. I was the one hired! After getting the job, I worked so hard and was recognized for my work ethic. I used this recognition as an opportunity to get Sharon, my American friend who had not been hired, an interview and a job. My foreign privilege secured me the job I wanted.

Not too soon after, I would experience being on the other side of privilege: being singled out and rejected, ironically, for the same quality that had gotten me hired: being African.

"I don't want no colored girl." That's what the nursing home resident said after one look at me. It was the first time I had even been called by that term. I didn't even realize how terrible it was until I told my friend Sharon what he said. Her jaw dropped and tears came to her eyes. "Oh, Lyna, are you okay? Girl, you need to go to HR." HR? I thought. What am I going to say to HR? That a resident refused my care? It sounded like something I would get in trouble for.

"No, girl," Sharon said. "He shouldn't be calling you that."

However, when I told the nurse leader in charge what the man said, she just removed the elderly resident from my assignment and assigned me a different resident. To her, everything was business as usual. No one in leadership checked on me to see how I was feeling. Only my friend cared. That was my first experience with American racism.

Vestiges of an Inhumane History

I left my job at the nursing home a few months after the incident, but the experience stuck with me. It wasn't just the man's racism or the pain and confusion I felt when he rejected me even though I had done nothing to him. I realized that I still had so much to learn about the history of my new country. In high school, I didn't learn much about American history because foreign history was an elective and I had opted for geography. So, the painful truths shocked me when I finally came across them.

Among the most unsettling things I learned about was the transatlantic slave trade. People from Africa were captured, chained to each other, and then arranged and loaded as cargo in sea vessels! Some of the captives were familiar with each other and perhaps spoke each other's languages, while some were strangers and could not communicate. The sea vessels kept their "cargo" in horrible, inhumane conditions! It took months to travel to their destinations in the west. Some of these captive Africans died on the way, and while some bodies were thrown into the sea, most of the time, the living had to sleep with and smell the rotting corpses! The captives went without food, water, or treatment when they got ill. When they arrived in America, they were officially and legally enslaved!

Women were raped by their captors and owners! People of all ages were traded, sold, and bequeathed as inheritances! Babies were ripped out of their mother's arms and sold to separate slave "owners," never to meet again! The more I learned, the more I could not believe it was real. No one in power cared about the pain and suffering of these human beings. As a matter of fact, they got whipped and punished if they did not hand over their baby to its new enslaver. These Africans endured horrible psychological, physical, emotional, and mental trauma. They lost their languages. They lost their traditions. They lost their customs. They had to learn English or French or Spanish or Portuguese, new languages necessary to communicate with their enslavers and each other. They were assigned new names, mostly one name, and had to take their enslaver's surname. They were denied information and education. It was illegal to learn to read! If caught, they were severely punished, as were the people who taught them.

Yet, I learned, their spirits were not broken despite living in horrendous conditions. They taught themselves how to read and write, some using the enslaver's children's books. Some learned by eavesdropping when those children were taught. They then taught each other how to read and write. They became innovative and creative, using their hair and quilts and songs to communicate escape routes. Can you believe their resilience? They shaped American society and culture in ways that we still do not entirely understand or appreciate.

At all points in this devastating history, some leaders emerged and spoke up and fought these practices and policies of enslavement. Other leaders joined them in the abolition movement. It took leaders who held power and privilege to use that power and privilege to abolish slavery. It's a difficult, painful history, but we study it so we don't repeat it. We learn so we can understand who we are as leaders and how our power and privilege affect those we serve. We learn it to know who not to become and what we can prevent. Most importantly, we learn history to recognize and identify biases from those histories that still affect us today. Fortunately, we always have opportunities to turn our power and privilege into activism and allyship to create a positive impact.

Residues of History

Here are some examples of types of oppression still prevalent today. They continue because power and privilege are being misused to exploit others. Reflect on these examples as you read through and recall that cultural humility challenges us to acknowledge our power and privilege and recognize that they positively or negatively affect those we serve. Inclusivity means using our power and privilege to elevate humanity above the "isms" described below. Arguably, inherent in power and privilege is also an obligation to do no harm, to do good, and to heal.

Racism

In matters of race, even though the global majority is non-White, in the United States, the White people are the majority. They created systems and drafted a constitution that favors the White settlers. At some point, the enslaved Africans were not viewed as full human but three fifths or fraction of a person. This was for economic power and privilege purposes. The disadvantaged groups experience racism, a type of oppression where White, European-descent people hate, prejudge, and discriminate non-White people solely based on having pigmented skin color. We have heard of the ideology of White supremacy, an ideology that anything White or of European descent is good or superior while anything non-White is inferior or not good enough. Unconsciously, even non-White people embrace this ideology where teachers or doctors have looked down on Black students or patients. Recently, an African American physician went to the bank to deposit a $16,000 check. The bank clerk could not believe that it was her check or that it was legitimate despite calling her employer to verify. The bank staff assumed the Black female customer could neither be a doctor nor afford to have that amount of money. Despite the doctor showing them her work medical doctor identification and calling her work to confirm her identity, the bank humiliated and inconvenienced her. The story, like many others, made national news. We need to continue mitigating the effects of our racial biases to become antiracist.

Ableism

This can refer to both mental and physical ability. The able-bodied groups have advantages over the people with visible or invisible disabilities. Those with disabilities are judged or denied opportunities because they may be assumed incapable of effectively performing certain tasks or roles. It is also when you use ableist language, such as assuming that your colleague is faking disability or acting like disability does not exist. For example, stating to a coworker, "You do not look disabled" just because their disability is invisible, is a form of ableism.

Ageism

Middle-aged adults are the favored group when it comes to age, while children, youth, and the elderly are considered disadvantaged. Some age-related microaggressions include: "You could be my daughter/son," "You don't have any experience," and "You are too young to qualify for that job/role." We have heard of stories where companies laid off older workers while they hired younger ones whom they paid lower salaries. During the COVID-19 pandemic, we witnessed the deaths of many elderly people in nursing homes or residential facilities. While most elderly persons are immunocompromised, some advocates argue that the elderly are often neglected and discarded because they are no longer contributing to the economy.

Sexism

Assigned sex at birth affects women because our social systems and traditions are male-dominated and influenced. Sexism is seen when women are considered less qualified than men and unfit for certain roles. We live in a society where women are paid less, denied leadership opportunities, or may be fired due to pregnancy. We have also heard stories where interviewers questioned women about pregnancy or daycare plans while their male peers were not or cases where women are interrupted during a speech or not given an opportunity to make a point together.

Homophobia

Our society has been comfortable with heterosexual, male and female relationships. Any relationship configuration outside this "norm" is seen as bad or unusual. Same-sex marriage was legalized in the United States in 2015. I remember being at church one weekend when the preacher from the pulpit pronounced, "Homosexuality is sin. God hates sin. If you are gay or homosexual, you are going to hell!" This was an uncomfortable and exclusive message to some. Clearly, this was a hostile and harmful environment for anyone who is not bothered by whom people choose to love.

Religious Oppression

There are many world religions. However, in the US, the protestants or evangelicals are the majority. The other groups, such as Jews, Muslims, Hindus, or Catholics, may experience religious oppression through exclusion. For example, most malls play Christmas music at the end of the year. The other groups don't have a choice but to listen to it. A Muslim woman wearing a hijab may be stereotyped as a terrorist and targeted with hate crimes by certain groups. While Christian prayer is welcome and seen as usual in most public places, other religions are not quite as embraced. Did you know there are 19 holidays between December and January celebrated by different people?

Classism

People in one group own homes and hold managerial positions in their work. The other groups are wage workers or the poor working class. When we stereotype working-class people as poor, bad, and less intelligent, we are operating in classism. For example, when teachers fail or unfairly grade students simply by assuming that students don't have time or support to study because their parents are homeless or rent in poor low-income neighborhoods, that is classism. Also, when we treat high-income people better than those with low income, that is classism.

Xenophobia

This refers to the fear of foreigners. Individuals born in the United States may treat those born outside the country as foreign. We have seen the term "illegal aliens" used to describe immigrants and, in a more extreme example, former U.S. President Donald Trump called Mexican immigrants "criminals and rapists." This is xenophobia. Further, in the US, White people have seen themselves as the "true" Americans, and anyone from a minoritized ethnic group, even if their ancestors had been here before a White person's ancestors, might still be considered foreign and treated with xenophobia. Many African Americans are descended from people who were kidnapped to the United States hundreds of years ago and carry a far longer legacy than some White Americans. Yet, we have leaders in congress say statements like "Go back where you came from" to other leaders they view as un-American. While we have come a long way, there is a lack of representation of the Native Americans in the leadership of the country.

Linguistic Oppression

This occurs when speakers of a language look down on people whose native language is different. English is the dominant language in the United States, and those who speak broken or accented English may be considered ignorant and unintelligent. This prejudice may affect job opportunities or cause someone to be denied professional development because of the assumption of relating an accent with poor leadership or unqualified. Some teachers may poorly grade those students who speak a different native language, forgetting that those students may already speak several languages and that English may be a second or third language for them. I have also noticed times when leaders are assumed not to know so their ideas are ignored because they have an accent.

Elitism

This "ism" is based on the level of education or the hierarchy of your education in society. In other countries, like Kenya, "elite" means that one is wealthy, regardless of level of education. In America, the elite concept means college-educated people are considered elite compared to those without a degree. Further, those who attended Ivy League universities get better and more opportunities than those who attended public or less prestigious schools. This is especially true of leadership in political or governmental institutions.

Militarism

This arises from various branches of the military viewing other groups as less significant. For example, World War II and Korean War veterans looking down on Vietnam or Gulf War veterans. Similarly, Marines are more favorably treated than veterans from other military branches. Further, members of the military may consider themselves morally superior to civilians. Some companies may or may not hire military veterans over civilian candidates.

Rankism

This happens when one level of a profession is seen as more important, smarter, and better than another. For instance, registered nurses are viewed as the standard. Those at the practical nursing level or nursing assistant level are treated poorly due to their level in the profession. Nurses with higher or advanced degrees in practice, such as a doctor of nursing practice (DNP), look down on those with a research degree, such as a PhD. There is also another example where registered nurses who become leaders yet look down on clinical practice or "bedside" nurses. These are examples within the nursing profession. Have you seen this in your profession?

Sizeism

The advantaged group is made up of those with a smaller body size which is presumed favorable. The disadvantaged group, those with large body sizes or who are overweight, miss opportunities because they are viewed less favorably. Studies show that those who are seen as attractive get hired or promoted compared to other groups. A few years ago, I flew to Kenya for my father's funeral. When checking in at the airport, the airline agent holding our family passports looked at the open passport in front of her and then studied my youngest baby in my husband's arms. "Are you sure that the child is 15 months old?" she asked. My first thought was to ask her what the passport said, but then I wondered, if this agent doesn't believe the federal government, how do I expect her to believe me? I politely said yes. As much as I wanted to educate her on her sizeism, I was exhausted and grieving. I wondered if her reaction would have been the same if my daughter had a smaller body size.

Whataboutism

When an advantaged group has power and is usually not affected in a situation, and the disadvantaged group is oppressed or affected and brings up their concern, the unaffected group dismisses the concerns by bringing up a different concern affecting them or a different group. For example, when talking about breast cancer, a colon cancer advocate argues that there are also concerns for colon cancer. When discussing police brutality against non-White people, as documented by the American Public Health Association, another group may bring up Black-on-Black crime. This is a logical fallacy in its purest form and operates as a way to deflect from discussing an uncomfortable topic to avoiding the issue altogether.

Tokenism

Tokenism happens when the majority of professionals in a company are from one advantaged group. They hire someone from a minoritized group for their own feel-good or savior mentality attitude. The new hire is not accorded the same privileges within the company. Therefore, they cannot really function as their authentic selves; instead, they are expected and must assimilate to the culture and get approval for their work or decisions. In other words, tokens are hired to check off a diversity box. For example, when a leader is hired as a token, they are neither allowed to fully function in their position nor exercise the authority that comes with their role because of resistance from those who hired them to or are tasked with leading.

Activate Your Power and Privilege into Allyship

People in leadership positions who value inclusivity work at all costs to prevent or avoid perpetrating or promoting such dehumanizing practices against others. We are challenged to recognize our power and privileges and realize that they affect those we serve, both for better and for worse. Leaders who value being inclusive prioritize using their privilege to do and magnify the humanity and potential of the people they serve. As leaders, we must be careful to perpetuate positive and compassionate leadership and not become that which we detest.

Standing Up as an Ally Maximizes Humanity

Here is a story of how a friend of mine saved a situation and met a new friend. Being her day off, she had to return something to a store and while there, did some more shopping. At the entrance to the fitting rooms, there were two people waiting to be admitted to a room: a young woman and my friend. They got their numbers and started walking towards the ladies' entrance. The associate attending to the fitting rooms stopped the young woman.

The associate said, "No, you can't go in there."

The young woman replied, "Why not?"

"You are not a girl."

"Yes, I am!" At this point, my friend realized this was about to take a negative turn so she stepped up and said, "Ma'am. But she has told you she is a girl. Why would you doubt her? Do you know her gender?"

The associate stammered, "But, but . . . but she looks like a boy to me."

My friend replied, "You say she looks like a boy, but she has assured you she is a girl."

"I don't know. I might have to call the manager."

My friend replied, "Ma'am, you don't have to call the manager. This is how you are going to create a scene and find your store in the news, and you don't want that. It's just me and her here as it is and I really do not have a problem. After all, she will be in her cube and me in mine."

Finally, the associate acquiesced, "Well, I guess you are right. You can go, too, young lady!"

> *My friend talked with her new friend, the girl, and they modeled their potential purchases for each other in the fitting room. The girl even went to the associate to ask her how she looked, and the associate smiled and told her she looked beautiful in red.*

My friend used her power and privilege, having a right to be in the dressing room as a female-appearing human, to advocate and speak up for a person who was profiled and treated poorly because of what she didn't "look like." My friend was the ally who made someone feel seen, heard, and valued, but the onus is on the company to train its staff to manage their biases so that this kind of exclusion never happens. That responsibility starts with its leadership. It starts with leaders who works to maximize our humanity.

The Necessity of Introspection

When we reflect upon and evaluate our feelings, actions, and decisions, we may recognize that our positions, titles, authority, and cultural background give us power and privilege. We should always aim to include others. We have a duty to make sure that people we interact with feel a sense of belonging.

Everyone can be an ally for someone. Each and every leader can advocate for another's needs, speak up against wrong, and/or extend an opportunity. As leaders, we can use our power and privilege as we please. We can stop being human, hurt and oppress people, or maximize our humanity so we can value and positively impact people. My hope is that we can activate our power and privilege into allyship, to do good.

Recognize Your Privilege

Try this activity. (*Adapted from (McIntosh, P. (1989). White privilege: Unpacking the Invisible Knapsack).*

You will need a packet of Skittles (or beans or beads), a cup, and a bowl.

- Pour the Skittles into a bowl.
- Have an empty cup ready.
- Below are lists of statements for several kinds of privilege we might enjoy.
- Read each statement, then answer "yes" or "no."
- For every "yes," take one Skittle from the bowl and put it in your cup.

Ability Privilege

- I can assume that I will easily have physical access to any building.
- I have never been taunted, teased, or ostracized due to a disability.
- I can do well in a challenging situation without being told I am an inspiration because of my ability status.
- I can go shopping alone and expect to find appropriate accommodation to make the experience hassle-free.
- I do not have to request accommodations due to my ability status.
- If I am not hired for a job, I do not question if it was due to my physical or mental ability.
- Other people do not think my mental ability is limited because of my physical ability.

Race Privilege

- Mainstream media routinely depict people of my race in a wide range of roles.
- Children in my racial groups do not need to be educated about systemic racism for their daily physical safety.
- I can be sure that if I need legal or medical help, my race will not work against me.
- I can take a job without people thinking I was hired only because of my race.
- I can do well in a challenging situation without being called a credit to my race.
- I am never asked to speak for all the people of my racial group.
- I can go shopping without concern that store employees will monitor me because of my race.

Gender Privilege

- If I have children and a successful career, few people will ask me how I balance work and home.
- I do not have to think about the message my wardrobe sends about my sexual availability.
- I never worry about being recognized as the sex/gender with which I identify.
- A decision to hire me will never be based on assumptions about whether or not I might plan to have a family soon.
- I am less likely to be sexually harassed at work than persons of other gender identities.
- In general, I am not under much pressure to be thin or to worry about how people will respond to me if I'm overweight.
- Major religions in the world are led mainly by people of my sex.

Sexuality Privilege

- I have formalized or could formalize my love relationship legally through marriage.
- I can move about in public without fear of being harassed or physically attacked because of my sexual identity.
- I do not have to fear negative consequences if my coworkers find out about my sexual identity.
- If I want to, I can easily find a religious community that welcomes persons of my sexual identity.
- No one questions the "normality" of my sexual identity.
- People don't ask me why I "chose" my sexual identity.
- I easily can find sex education literature about my sexual identity.

Nationality Privilege (U.S.)

- If I apply for a job, my legal right to work in this country probably will not be questioned.
- I will never be denied housing in the U.S. due to my citizenship.
- I can go into any bank and set up a checking account without fear of discrimination.
- I can be reasonably sure that if I need legal and medical assistance, my citizenship status will not matter.
- I do not fear that my employer will threaten me with deportation.
- I wanted to; I could travel freely to any country and be admitted back to the U.S.
- If I were a victim of a crime, I wouldn't think twice about seeking police assistance due to my citizenship status.

Class Privilege

- I can be sure that my social class will be an advantage when I seek medical or legal help.
- I am fairly certain that I will not have to skip meals because I cannot afford to eat.
- I have a savings account with at least a month's expenses in case of emergency.
- In case of a medical emergency, I won't have to decide against visiting a doctor or hospital due to economic reasons.
- I don't have to rely on public transportation; I can afford my own vehicle.
- My neighborhood is relatively free of obvious drug use, prostitution, and violent crime.
- Most experts appearing in mass media seem to be from my social class.

Religious Privilege

- I can assume that I will not have to work or go to school on my religious holidays.
- I can be sure that the mainstream media will celebrate the holidays of my religion.
- My religious views are reflected by the majority of government officials and political candidates.
- Food that honors my religious practices can be easily found in any restaurant or grocery store.
- Places to worship or practice my religion are numerous in my community.
- Most people do not consider my religious practices to be "weird."
- I don't need to worry about the negative consequences of disclosing my religious identity to others.

Now that you have completed the activity, look at your cup of Skittles. You can also compare your collection of Skittles to other participants. The number of skittles shows your privilege.

Where are you most privileged?
Where are you least privileged?
What surprised you the most?

Notice that you can be more or less privileged in different areas. Everyone can be an ally for someone. It is a matter of choice. Once you know your privilege, speak up and out against injustices. We can politely but firmly call out those ignoring or interrupting others in meetings so we can amplify the voices of those being ignored or silenced. We can assess our systems and create opportunities for everyone. When in a position of power and privilege, activate allyship and solve for inclusion to give the marginalized, minoritized, underprivileged, underrepresented, and underserved persons a sense of belonging.

_____

_____

_____

_____

_____

_____

_____

_____

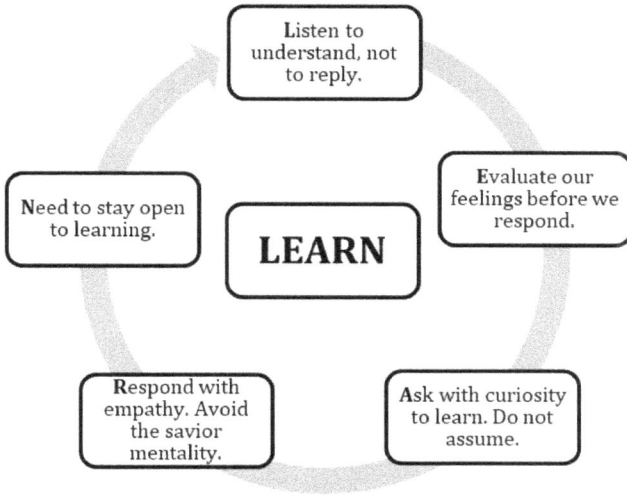

Listen to understand, not to reply.

Need to stay open to learning.

LEARN

Evaluate our feelings before we respond.

Respond with empathy. Avoid the savior mentality.

Ask with curiosity to learn. Do not assume.

TAKEAWAYS

- When we forget our shared humanity, we can too easily abuse our power and privilege and harm marginalized, and minoritized individuals.
- When we maximize our humanity, we utilize our power and privilege to do right and become allies who create a positive impact.

CALL TO LEARN

- Reflect on how your actions may intentionally or unintentionally be oppressing those you interact with.
- Complete the privilege activity. Who needs your allyship?

MISTAKE #3

Believing people are too easily offended or overly sensitive.

PRACTICE

3

Practice Inclusive Communication

To effectively communicate, we must realize that we are all different in the way we perceive the world and then use this understanding as a guide to our communication with others. —Tony Robbins

Definitions

I was chatting with a colleague who mentioned that his family immigrated some 20 years ago from Romania to the United States. He was born into communism and raised by Christian parents. He remembers the government was very oppressive to Christians, who often protested on the streets. No matter your background, most marginalized people are often oppressed and silenced, so the privileged people don't feel offended or inconvenienced. As leaders, we need to be aware of how our communication, intentional or unintentional, might harm others. First, we must learn history. The Spanish philosopher George Santayana once said, "Those who cannot remember the past are condemned to repeat it," while the British statesman Winston Churchill wrote, "Those that fail to learn from history are doomed to repeat it." Second, we must identify who the marginalized groups are. Third and last, we must recognize how we affect others.

In the spirit of effective communication, as you read this book, I would like to make sure we have the same definitions for context purposes. To understand and effectively apply the inclusive practices shared in this book, let us start by reflecting on the historical background of the United States. Some people have been unfairly treated or discriminated against because of their skin color, ability, age, gender, nationality, religion, education, economic, social status, or simply geographic location. These people are also known as marginalized or minoritized groups. The work of diversity, equity, and inclusion was started to support people from marginalized, minoritized, disadvantaged, underprivileged, underrepresented, and underserved groups. Therefore, for DEIB work to succeed, every initiative must center around these groups. Below are some definitions of the words and ideas I use in this book:

An **antiracist** is, according to antiracism researcher Ibram X. Kendi, "One who is supporting an antiracist policy through their actions or expressing an antiracist idea."

Belonging is seeing, hearing, and respecting people, which leads them to feel safe, secure, and supported. Belonging happens when equity and inclusion are achieved.

Black refers to a racialized classification of people of African ancestry based on skin color or pigmentation regardless of the wide range of skin shades from light to dark brown.

Cultural bias is when we view or perceive other cultures as bad, sad, painful, less than, or not good enough compared to our own. We can also have cultural biases that elevate another culture as superior to our own.

Cultural competence is a process that offers information, usually basic, superficial, and generalized knowledge, about a group or population from a single perspective, a Western perspective, which tends to scientifically order and label the world into categories and traits.

Cultural humility is a concept coined in 1998 by two doctors, Melanie Tervalon and Jann Murray-Garcia. It is a three-part framework that includes self-reflection, recognizing power imbalances, and being open to the continuous process of learning.

A **cultural humility approach** refers to practicing cultural humility by listening to understand, asking with curiosity while acknowledging feelings and biases, recognizing power and privilege imbalances in our interactions, and being open to learning new ideas or perspectives.

Culture shock refers to the impact of moving from a familiar culture to one that is unfamiliar. This impact includes the anxiety and feelings (such as surprise, disorientation, uncertainty, and confusion) felt when a person must adapt to a different and unknown cultural or social environment.

DEIB stands for diversity, equity, inclusion, and belonging.

A **disadvantaged person** is a member of a community that has historically experienced discrimination based on differences beyond their control, such as race, sex, location, poverty, disability, ethnicity, language, migration, and displacement and which negatively affects their well-being. The discrimination results in people living in geographical locations that face environmental pollution, have low income, have high unemployment, high rent burdens, low levels of home ownership, or low levels of educational attainment and remain in cycles of low economic resources.

Diversity is our differences, visible or invisible, acknowledged, accepted or otherwise. It is also a deviation from the societal "norm." In this book, diversity refers to the marginalized, minoritized, disadvantaged, underprivileged, underrepresented, and underserved groups.

The **dominant group** is the controlling or influential group either by having more population or power.

Equity is identifying, acknowledging, and meeting a person's unique needs. To achieve equity, we must find out the needs of our diverse teams and meet them uniquely.

Inclusion is inviting, embracing, and fully accepting people's unique differences and taking action to meet their unique needs by seeing, hearing, and respecting them. It is acknowledging that we are different, intentionally being aware of and embracing those differences, and unconditionally accepting them.

LGBTQ+ encompasses lesbian, gay, bisexual, transgender, and questioning people.

Marginalized people or groups have more obstacles when accessing basic rights or services. The obstacles are due to systemic or social exclusion.

Microaggression is an intentional or unintentional word or gesture that is hurtful or stigmatizing to marginalized or minoritized people. For example, some people say to me, "You speak very good English for an African."

Microinsult is a word or action that is intended to be rude to express insensitivity and demean a person's racial background. Often it comes from a stereotypical place. For example, a physician, while conducting a college intake physical, asks a Black student if they got admitted into university because of affirmative action.

Minoritized people or groups are those who have been made to be or labeled subordinate (or less than) by a dominant group.

Oppression is the power to exact unjust or cruel treatment or control over people.

People of global majority refers to people who have been racialized or labeled as minorities. It is a collective term referring to people of non-European ancestry. In the United States, this includes Black, Brown, Asian, Native Americans and bi- or multiracial people.

People of global minority refers to people who are racialized or labeled as the majority or of European ancestry in the United States.

Power is the capacity to direct or influence how others behave or the course of events.

Privilege is defined by the Oxford English Dictionary as "a special right, earned or unearned advantage, or immunity granted or available only to a particular person or group." In this book, privilege refers to the *lack of barriers or obstacles* one has in life when accessing or attempting to access basic services.

Racism is a socially constructed idea claiming that different races have distinct characteristics, abilities, or qualities so as to distinguish them as inferior or superior to one another. This results in discrimination or prejudice against certain minoritized or marginalized groups which denies them opportunities or access to basic services.

A **racist** is, according to Kendi, "One who is supporting a racist policy through their actions or inaction or expressing a racist idea" (p.13).

A **stereotype** is a widely believed fixed and oversimplified image or idea of a particular type of person or thing. For example, there is a widely fixed assumption that leadership roles are for men and women belong in subordinate roles. Or that Black people are lazy.

Unconscious biases are also known as implicit biases.

Underrepresented groups are groups of people whose representation is disproportionately smaller compared to their numbers in the general population. For example, in the United States, these are people of the global majority, with different abilities, of lower socioeconomic status, the LGBTQ+ group, the nondominant religion, women, or older people of retirement age.

White refers to a racialized classification of people of European ancestry based on skin color that lacks pigmentation.

White privilege is the status of having fewer or no obstacles to overcome in life, owing to having lighter skin.

Use Inclusive Language

Effective communication is a necessary skill that requires and takes practice. In the words of Tony Robbins, "To effectively communicate, we must realize that we are all different in the way we perceive the world and then use this understanding as a guide to our communication with others." For the leaders in the human service industry, inclusive communication means sharing information in a way that each unique individual understands.

This means communicating from a cultural humility by recognizing that each person communicates differently and then giving a person opportunities and resources so they can freely and fully express themselves to make their needs known. There are many ways to communicate, such as using language, signs, verbal, and non-verbal means.

On the other hand, ineffective communication excludes and can lead to discrimination. In our interactions, we might unintentionally use language, words or behaviors that hurt or exclude others. For example, a word or gesture might be insulting, a well-meaning joke might be inappropriate, or an intended compliment from one person could be a microaggression to another. According to the Merriam-Webster dictionary, a microaggression is a comment or action that subtly and often unconsciously or unintentionally expresses a prejudiced attitude toward a member of a marginalized group. Microaggressions are often directed at people from marginalized or minoritized groups. For example, some people say to me, "You speak very good English for an African!" While it is true that I have a different English accent, the stereotype in this statement is an assumption that Africans do not speak English or that the English language is for non-Africans. Most people are surprised to learn that 26 African countries use English as their official language.

Examples of Microaggressions

Marginalized Group	Microaggression	Directed at
Race	He is so articulate for a Black man.	African American male
Ability	You don't look disabled	Person with an invisible disability
Sexual Orientation	That is so gay!	Two people showing affection publicly

Marginalized Group	Microaggression	Directed at
Religious Oppression	It is so hot, are you going to keep wearing that headdress?	Muslim female wearing a hijab
Class	Do you need free food?	African American female at a fast-food restaurant.
Nationality	Are you Chinese?	Asian Appearing person
Race	I don't see color	Person of the global majority
Education	They didn't teach you that in school?	College-educated person
Language	(Talking loudly and very slowly)	A person with an accent other than the local accent

Have you experienced any microaggressions? Were you aware of the ones on the list above? As subtle as they may seem, micro-aggressions and stereotypes weigh heavily on the receiver's mind. Studies show that internalizing stereotypes affects our mental health. Unfortunately, those who perpetrate the microaggression may not see it as a big deal so they dismiss any concerns, which is like adding insult to injury. This denial that they have caused harm is also known as gaslighting. For example, after being made aware of their microaggression, the person may argue that since they had good intentions, the receivers should not be offended.

Leaders need to recognize that microaggressions create a toxic and oppressive environment. In such environments, the marginalized end up missing work because they are emotionally and mentally stressed. This type of ineffective and discrimina-tory communication affects their mental health, which leads to avoidable use of sick days and loss of revenue. To avoid hurting or excluding people means being mindful of your language and aware that even well-meaning words, behaviors, or gestures can harm others. Cultural humility challenges us to learn more about inclusive language, words, behaviors, and gestures.

Words (and Gestures) Matter

Words are powerful. Inclusive leaders use inclusive language because they know that words can empower the weakest and destroy the toughest. Inclusive language, terms, and expressions make people feel welcome and included. On the other hand, exclusive language makes individuals feel unwelcome or excluded. A cultural humility approach reminds us to reflect on the language we use so we can engage in conversations with empathy. We must also be humble enough to listen and learn not to gaslight others. It's difficult to understand and meet people's needs unless we ask them. When we fail to ask, we end up with false conclusions and inaccurate assumptions about those we are trying to help and serve.

Non-verbal communication or gestures are just as powerful and effective as the use of language or words. Our unconscious biases show up in our gestures and behaviors. I was facilitating a leadership workshop where one participant shared that one evening when he was in high school, he went to visit his friend but couldn't find him at his home. So, he decided to go back to his house. While he was walking back to his house, he saw someone walking toward him in the opposite direction. There was a bit of distance between them so he could not really tell who it was. However, as they got closer, he could tell it was a Black person and decided to cross the street to walk away because he was afraid. As they got closer and were about to pass each other, he realized the Black stranger he was afraid of was his friend who had gone to his house to visit him. As they called each other and ran to hug one another, he was embarrassed and ashamed. He never shared this story until that day at the workshop.

Upon reflecting, he explained that while walking, when he passed people who were White like him, he didn't cross the street to avoid them because he didn't feel afraid. This is a perfect example of an exclusive gesture, a non-verbal microaggression. Unfortunately, we all have biases; we just need to manage them by reflecting on and adapting inclusive practices.

I also have learned that gestures are not universal. For example, nodding your head is not a universal yes, rather an indication of acknowledgment. A firm handshake is only possible when you have hands or do not have a medical condition that prevents you from having a strong hand grip. Asking everyone to join you by standing and clapping assumes that everyone can stand and is capable of clapping. Other gestures, such as a thumbs-up, may mean something completely different from one culture to another. Being mindful of those we interact with and taking time to learn and avoid exclusive gestures are intentional efforts to be an ally and show care and respect for others.

Recently, someone asked why I chose to include pronouns on my LinkedIn profile. I told her it was my simple demonstration of allyship. We had a discussion where some people argued that they don't need to show their pronouns, while others said they feel it is important to do so. For others, especially those with unisex names, having the pronouns avoids any confusion and guarantees proper identification. Others who self-identify as a particular gender feel it is important to have their pronouns for easy identification. Considering the ways people from the lesbian, gay, bisexual, transgender, and questioning (LGBTQ) community have been marginalized in the workplace, I and many others see this as an opportunity to be an ally. Some members of the LGBTQ community have mentioned that they see their allies and know that they are safe around people who have self-identified using their pronouns. Talk about small intentional gestures of inclusion.

Always Be Ready to Revisit Your Assumptions

At a neuroscience conference, Joe, an executive, mentioned that he had spoken with his future business partners many times over the phone and virtually. When it was time to close the deal, he flew to sign the partnership contract with his new business partner. As soon as he arrived in the conference room to meet his partners, he stretched his hand out for a handshake, as he considered it standard business etiquette. He was confused when his new partner did not put out his hand. As a reflex, he thought the deal would not go through. But after gathering himself and focusing on the partner sitting in front of him, he realized that his new partner had no hands. He immediately apologized. He then went into reflection mode. Even after several phone conversations, he never visualized a person with a disability. He had automatically assumed that the partner would have hands. From this experience, we understand that gestures, while often cultural, are not universal for everyone. In the instances that they are not, we need to revisit our assumptions and adapt to the new context.

At its core, to be inclusive means to never assume. Instead, think about your audience, the context, and the times, and solve for impact, not just intent. Remember, inclusive communication takes practice. Some people may disagree with some terms or gestures, which is perfectly okay. That disagreement is part of how language and communication shift toward new meanings and, ideally, better inclusivity. Always be honest, truthful, and mindful. Acknowledging people's differences and preferences is valuing who they are. It allows people to feel a sense of belonging. This will not only make them feel seen and respected but also definitely improve your relationships.

Examples of How Language Shifts

Language As It Was	Language Evolving	Cultural Humility
Hey guys	Hey ladies and gentlemen	Hey everyone
Wo/Mankind	Humankind	Ask
My fellow	My colleagues	Ask
Boys and Girls	Students or class	Ask
Use blues and pinks	Use all crayon colors	Ask
I am bipolar	I have bipolar	Ask
I am diabetic	I have diabetes	Ask
Handicapped	Persons with disabilities	Ask
Autistic kids	Kids on the autism spectrum	Ask
Special Needs kids	Kids with developmental disabilities	Ask
The blind	People with vision impairment	Ask
The deaf	People with hearing impairment	Ask
Crippled	People with physical disabilities	Ask
The dumb	People with verbal disabilities	Ask
Suffering from	Battling a disease	Ask
Victim of	Survivor of	Ask

How Does Cultural Humility Support Communication?

I once heard a colleague describe an "expert" as someone who knows so much about so little, and I think that characterization applies here. When it comes to the work of DEIB, language is constantly changing, and it remains both broad and specialized. While all DEIB leaders are qualified in general matters of equity, inclusion and belonging, we are not experts in every area. It is important we acknowledge not knowing everything and seeking to not only listen to others but learn from those who are well versed in that subject. It is necessary to seek an anti-racist scholar to get the most current and acceptable language when addressing race matters. To learn the up-to-date language on disability studies, ask a disability language expert. To learn more about gender-inclusive language, seek information from a gender studies specialist, or if we want to gain knowledge on what's acceptable in a specific gender, such as transgender, cisgender, intergender, or non-binary community, then ask experts in those communities.

As a matter of good practice, even when the expert says the right terminology, still ask a person what they prefer to be called or how they like to be addressed. This is because an expert may be aware of general terms that most often do not represent the unique individual. On the other hand, an individual's unique preference is not representative of whatever group they may be associated with. To effectively and inclusively communicate, focus on the unique individuals we are addressing so we can identify and meet their needs.

We hear most people say, "I was raised to treat people the same way I want to be treated." What I have learned is don't treat people how you would like to be treated. This is often based on assumptions that they like what you like. This stems from a position of power, control, and savior mentality. Instead treat people how they would like to be treated. This means you focus on the person you are interacting with. It means you see that person as a unique individual then out of respect, ask them how they would like to be treated. In the end it is about them. And you know what? It only takes one question and a change in one word. A cultural humility approach asks each human how they like to be treated. This is how you create cultures in any context where each individual feels respected and valued.

When we recognize people as unique individuals, we ask a person what they prefer to be called and their appropriate terminology or identity. Inclusive communication takes practice and a lifetime of learning. The best practice is to avoid gender-exclusive words or gender-specific colors and replace them with gender-neutral ones. Use your power and privilege to create safe spaces for the marginalized or minoritized so they do not have to suppress who they are. Effective inclusive leaders do not assume; they intentionally use inclusive language and a cultural humility approach to be self-aware and focus on the human they are interacting with. Inclusive communication is a necessary resource for building lasting relationships, being an ally and becoming an inclusive leader. It is a powerful practice that makes people feel welcome, safe, secure, and supported.

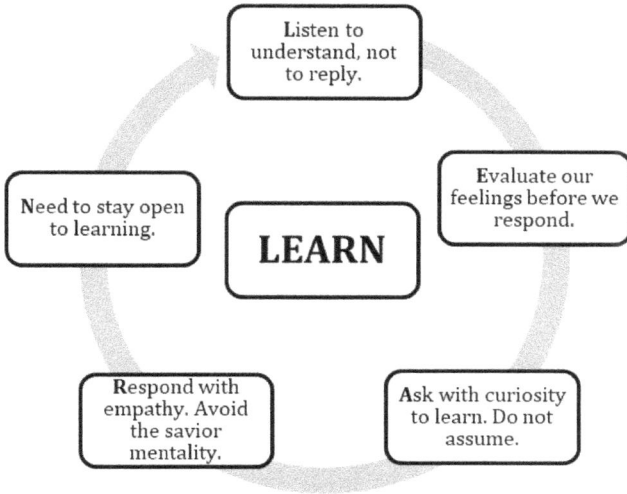

TAKEAWAYS

- Avoid assumptions by asking to learn what is acceptable to each unique human.
- Do not be a bystander. Be an agent of change.

CALL TO LEARN

- When an individual makes you aware of your microaggression, don't dismiss them or tell them they are overreacting.
- Ask a person how they prefer to be addressed.

MISTAKE #4

Why hire for diversity? I do not see color anyway.

PRACTICE

4

Focus on Inclusion

It is not our differences that divide us. It is our inability to recognize, accept, and celebrate those differences. —Audre Lorde

Being "Colorblind" is Not Inclusive

At a professional development training for college leaders, I overheard a group of leaders bragging about how their teams are diverse at a small group activity session. One male leader described how his company is 50% women. Hearing this, another leader asked him how many women of color work for him. He responded that he didn't know because he "doesn't see color." What does it mean when a person says that they "don't see color?" What was he really saying? This is a statement I often hear when I am leading workshops or training, and to me, they are a red flag. Such stories indicate a disconnect between what the leaders think and how their employees feel.

I have heard many leaders say they hired diverse employees or many employees of color. Many proudly declare their company the most diverse or tout all they have done for communities of color. However, when I speak with their employees, most do not share their leader's excitement. They often tell me a very different story:

"Lyna, what do you do when you are hired to be seen but not heard?"

"I am grateful to have a job, but I don't feel seen."

"I have ideas, but no one ever hears them."

"My colleagues get invited to attend conferences, but I do not. I have never been asked to attend, and when I asked, I was told there is no budget for it."

"I once prepared a huge presentation. After I shared it with my mentor, he told me it was a better idea if he presented it by himself."

"I have been passed up many times for leadership roles because I am told that I am a woman with young children."

"I have been told I am too young, so I need more experience before I become a director."

"I have been called too aggressive or too outspoken."

"Last Christmas, the director gave wine to everyone in our department. As a recovering alcoholic, that was very traumatizing."

"Oh, I remember the wine gift. As a Muslim, I didn't feel seen because my religious preferences were ignored."

All these statements are from employees of equal opportunity companies. Regardless of what the organization's leadership may believe about its policies, practices, and efforts, these statements show that the employees do not feel seen, heard, or valued. They show that DEIB work is still needed. Fortunately, with the right approach, every employee can have a sense of belonging—but leaders must first recognize that effective leadership is intentional and cultures of belonging take time and effort to build.

I have stated that we cannot solve a problem we do not recognize. Can you answer the question: What is your organization's diversity and inclusion outlook?

Leaders affect people either positively or negatively. The relationship is always charged, one way or another. Because they

hold power, there is no neutral ground in the relationship between a leader and their followers. To address persistent racial
tension, bring an end to centuries-old gender inequalities, and
stop discriminatory practices based on religion, age, class, and
ability, leaders need to prioritize becoming more inclusive. We
need leaders who are unafraid of speaking up and doing right to
correct injustices while honoring great practices in their organizations. Leaders who recognize that it is not enough to invest in
recruiting and hiring strategies but necessary to invest in training,
development, and retention strategies. We need to realize that
diversity alone will not promote equity or inclusion. Intentional
actionable items such as asking hard questions, developing measurable tools, and evaluating your inclusive strategies affect your
outcomes. I cannot overstate this point. Most leaders in organizations think that hiring employees of the global majority, the
non-White employees, is going to magically "fix" racism in the
workplace. However, hiring diverse employees is only a first step.

Hiring for "Diversity" Kudos Harms All Employees

*I was consulting at a company that was very excited be-
cause they had recently hired their first Black vice president. The company was so proud of increasing company
diversity, and the newly minted vice president told me that
she was also not only excited but grateful to have qualified for such an important role. After training for her role
and getting settled in her new office, she was informed that
she could not make any decisions independently, even as
the top leader of her department, without approval from
another leader from a different department. There is nothing wrong with having a mentor or someone to bounce off
ideas—until she realized she was the only one for whom*

this practice was required and expected. Did I mention that she learned that the other leader had no expertise or experience in her department and was fairly new to the organization? Confused, she decided to pursue the issue further with her leadership. Her boss told her that since she was new in leadership, even though she was a seasoned employee, it was in the company's best interest to have someone supervise her to prevent any mistakes that might hurt her or the company's image.

As the only woman of color in her department, she was not only offended but made to question their motives. It was as though they didn't trust her judgment; they expected her to make mistakes. This could be interpreted to mean the other leader was qualified to grade and approve her decisions despite the fact that she had met all the qualifications, was more seasoned, and had been at the company longer. In this case, hiring her was inviting diversity into the company. Recognizing and respecting her position is inclusion. Allowing her to exercise her authority in her role and listening and valuing her ideas would have given her a sense of belonging. If you guessed that this leader was demoralized, you are correct. If you think that she became disengaged, you thought right. And if you guessed that she was motivated to stay with this company, you are wrong. She decided to leave because the company's lack of trust and discriminatory practices created a toxic work environment. Unfortunately, she is not the only one who has been hired to brag about diversity but faced double standards or unfair treatment on the job.

What if Leaders Used Cultural Humility

We must start to invest in recruiting and hiring employees of color, supporting and providing their growth and development opportunities, and creating retention strategies such as mentoring and evaluation. I have been a mentor for years for both students and leaders. I know that hiring inexperienced staff and supporting them with mentoring opportunities from experienced team members improves communication and promotes engagement. I also know that creating conversations with team members builds relationships, avoids surprise lawsuits, and promotes retention. Therefore, as leaders, we must recognize the diversity in the company and provide a safe and supportive environment that encourages and welcomes the truest form of authenticity. We should reflect on our background, culture, and experience to learn and manage biases that affect our actions and decisions.

People recognize their own diversity, that is, we all know when we deviate from the "norm" around us. Depending on the situation, any person can be diverse. They just need to know that others see, hear, and value them. They not only need a safe space to make mistakes but a brave environment to learn and respectfully speak their minds. Inclusive environments embrace diversity and focus on finding commonalities in their teams or employees.

Years ago, I led training on a professional development day at a college. I asked the group what their institution's inclusion outlook was. Here is a response I got from one of the workshop participants:

As a White man, I joined the institution 15 years ago. At the time, we were only comprised of White, cis, straight folks at the top leadership level. Today, we have one Black director, one gay director, two White interim deans, one Black vice president, and one transgender female vice president. We still have a lot of work to do. However, I have seen years of tremendous change. You

*know what made the difference? Leadership made the difference.
It is that simple. I am the sole remaining executive at our
institution from 16 years ago. Diversity, equity, and inclusion is
hard work that needs us to work harder.*

After a short pause, the leader added, "Oh, and by the way,
I am the transgender female vice president. I finally found the
courage to be myself after hiding in shame all my life to come out
last year."

There are many stories like this one. Leadership made the
difference in that vice president's organization. Its leaders made
inclusivity the company's bottom line, and that decision influenced hiring and promotion decisions, improved retention, and
fostered a culture of belonging that rippled throughout the workplace. There are as many stories of exemplary leaders as there are
of despots. I have experienced them myself, including my Baba
herself, who fought for gender equality and against the arranged
marriages of children. She was a leader who stood for what she
believed in, even if it meant standing alone, and an advocate for
what was right. I wanted to be a leader like her. Leadership can
create a tremendous impact and lasting legacy.

Reflection: Why Isn't Diversity Enough?

When we focus on diversity alone, we identify only those things
that make each of us different from one another. We perpetuate
unconscious biases that lead to adverse outcomes. When we focus
on inclusion, we recognize our humanity and find commonalities
that lead to increased engagement by bringing together people
from different backgrounds who have diverse. Supporting people
in a safe and secure environment creates a culture of belonging.

Hiring for diversity is an easy, visible box to check, but team
members can easily become a token. Great leaders know that in-

clusive practices go beyond being an equal opportunity employer that hires diverse persons. Leaders should not only recruit and hire but also invest in inclusive training and developing their teams. They should develop standardized assessments to evaluate their employees, performance, and sense of belonging. They must apply inclusive practices that promote employee engagement by reaching out and asking employees to identify the support they need, what defines a sense of belonging *for them* and an inclusive work culture. Inclusion starts with us as leaders. Inclusion means we recognize all the differences in people, and we choose to focus on what we share so we can harness the power of our diversity as a whole. It also means we choose to ask and learn instead of assuming and concluding inaccurately.

An Equal Opportunity Company Doesn't Guarantee Equity

What about diversity without equity? What are some equitable strategies? Growing up, my grandmother used to tell the story of a man whose wife died and left him with a young daughter. The man went on to marry a beautiful woman who bore him two more daughters. Even though they lived in the same house, this stepmother was so mean to her stepdaughter that she made her the housemaid. She cooked, cleaned, and picked up after her family. However, she often went hungry and never got new clothes. Her story reminded me of the story of Cinderella, and it shows that being diverse in the same household goes beyond race—and it doesn't automatically mean you are welcome, included, or valued.

You may recall that Cinderella lived with her stepmother and stepsisters in a lovely home that was supposed to be an equal-opportunity environment while her father was alive. Unfortunately, once he passed away, Cinderella was forced to do all the housework while her sisters just relaxed with their mother.

Cinderella worked hard but was not appreciated or valued; indeed, she was exploited. The stepmother treated her as a servant and slave. Her sisters treated her like an outsider and refused to help her with chores. Her entire remaining family made her feel like she didn't belong. Her stepmother treated her unfairly and made sure she had had none of the privileges and opportunities her stepsisters had. When her sisters got new shoes and dresses to attend the ball at the king's palace, Cinderella could only watch their excitement. The stepmother, the leader, knew precisely what she was doing and saw nothing wrong with discriminating against Cinderella.

Then Cinderella's fairy godmother stepped in and asked what Cinderella wanted. The fairy godmother encouraged Cinderella to go to the ball and provided her with what she needed to get ready. When she arrived, Cinderella was noticed by the prince, who fell in love with her immediately and, after some hijinks with a missing shoe, invited her to be his princess.

Belonging: An Outcome of Equity and Inclusion

Take a moment to reflect and evaluate your leadership.
Are you like Cinderella's stepmother, who oppresses and explicitly excludes team members?
Are you the mentor or informal leader who acts as the fairy godmother to extend support and opportunities to your colleagues?
Are you the prince who is the leader in power that uses their power and privilege to uplift others?
Do you have certain employees that participate in some professional development activities while others are not allowed, either tacitly or explicitly?

Is your professional development budget inclusive and equitable to all your team members or only approved by those who are like you?

Do you encourage your team or employees to attend professional development trainings?

Do you extend opportunities for growth without judging or passing up your team from marginalized groups?

Great leaders should realize that diversity is an easy and highly visible box to check. However, being inclusive takes courage to shift mindsets and cultures that most company leaders do not even realize that they have *formed*. Unfortunately, we have seen many equal-opportunity companies make the choice to hire diverse employees but do not see the need to implement and evaluate their inclusive strategies. Each employee has unique needs. Meeting those needs will give them a sense of belonging. Hiring diverse teams is the easy part. Another easy part is that employees are aware of their diversity because that is who they are.

As visionaries, leaders are responsible for changing policies and creating spaces where people feel safe, secure and supported. As Richard Branson once said, "Train people well enough so they can leave. Treat them well enough, so they don't want to." With a cultural humility approach, inclusive leaders recognize, embrace appreciate, and celebrate diversity which in turn increases retention. Their employees are engaged because they are encouraged to share ideas and use their voices to make their needs known. *All*, not some, employees are offered training and development opportunities. Prioritizing equity demands that leaders ask that *one more question* with empathy so they can learn, save money and create excellent impact.

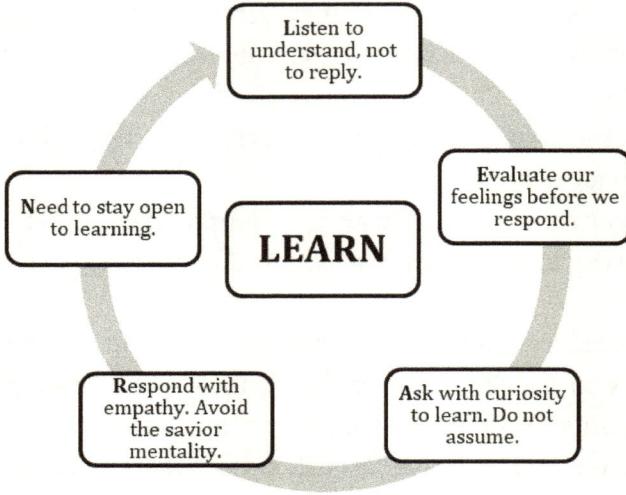

TAKEAWAYS

- Recognize and support the marginalized, minoritized, under-privileged, underrepresented, and underserved individuals in your organization.

CALL TO LEARN

- Identify and discuss the unique needs of your unique team members.
- Ask your team to rate their sense of belonging.

MISTAKE #5

As an equal opportunity employer, our focus is equality.

PRACTICE

5

Commit to Inclusion Excellence

We can't solve problems by using the same kind of thinking we used when we created them. —Albert Einstein

Cultural Humility is the Flip Side of Inclusive Excellence

When we are intentionally and actively doing the work of diversity, equity, and inclusion to ensure fairness and promote engagement, we are promoting inclusion excellence. Studies show that people don't leave jobs. They leave toxic work cultures, bad bosses, and improper or inadequate training. One study found that the top three reasons employees leave or change jobs are career development, work-life balance, and bad managers. It is encouraging to know that willing leaders can correct all those issues. People do not have to fall into these statistics—but this work starts with us.

An inclusive leader (and organization) should invest in recruiting, hiring, training, professional development, and offering work-life balance opportunities. These should be readily available and accessible resources to all employees. Unmanaged unconscious biases have been attributed to unfairly assigning or extending opportunities. Research shows that even well-intentioned people can unknowingly act in a manner that does not promote equity or inclusion. Leaders may extend opportunities to some, but perhaps not all, of their team members. Some make opportunities available but do not take time to listen to their team to learn whether the available resources are appropriate or relevant or outdated.

When leaders utilize a cultural humility to learn how to best serve their teams, this approach allows them to view their employees as unique individuals with unique needs who need to be valued and listened to. They, therefore, ensure that all those they serve have resources not only available but also *accessible* to them. Such leaders reflect on what they may not know about the people they serve and recognize how their power and influence affect them. They then listen and ensure that everyone's unique needs and goals are met.

Identifying a Bias Problem in the Field

A few years ago, a university consulted our company to address "some racial tension" that reportedly led to their students failing their nursing program. The university leader mentioned that he would like us to share our findings and recommendations with the students and the teachers. We set up faculty and student focus groups and listening sessions to obtain data and develop recommendations. We set up separate groups so we could establish safe and brave spaces for both groups. In the beginning, the students were hesitant to share their stories because they were afraid of retaliation or being failed. After a lot of reassurance, the students shared their stories of origin and voiced their concerns. They accused some of their instructors of assuming they were dumb, not ready for the college program, and not listening to them. We took notes and established facts: The students sought the university on their own. They voluntarily applied and were deemed qualified and admitted into the program. The students paid the university to be taught so they could graduate. They came from diverse origins and backgrounds with different experiences. Most importantly, they were vulnerable and did not have power or privilege in the classroom. On the other hand, the teachers expressed frustration that the students waited until the last minute or too late to communicate their concerns. They said that students didn't realize how tough and demanding the program would be, and instead, they complained among themselves instead of asking for assistance or guidance from the teachers. After several listening sessions and taking notes, we noted a few facts: The teachers are trained, therefore, qualified to teach. The teachers who voluntarily applied to the university were noted as qualified and hired. We also noted that the teachers were paid to teach so the students could graduate. The teachers had different backgrounds and origins and experienced culture differently. However, and most importantly, they were the leaders with power and privilege in the classroom,

The director's responsibility was to both the students and the teachers. The university could only be productive when the students and teachers had excellent performance. Therefore, the director had every reason to be concerned for the students as their sense or lack of belonging would affect the reputation of the college and economic welfare. He also had every intention of building a culture of belonging for both the students and teachers to ensure the university had standard achievement. The teachers had different backgrounds and origins and experienced culture differently. However, most importantly, they were the leaders with power and privilege in the classroom.

The director's responsibility was to both the students and

the teachers. The university could only be productive when the students and teachers had excellent performance. Therefore, the director had every reason to be concerned for the students as their sense or lack of belonging would affect the reputation of the college and economic welfare. He also had every intention of building a culture of belonging for both the students and teachers to ensure the university was an inclusive and equitable environment. By utilizing a cultural humility approach, he recognized the power imbalance and invested time and resources to create a culture of belonging.

How To Be a Supportive Leader

Consider a former colleague of mine, Linda, a director at our company for 10 years and one of the most effective leaders I've ever met. She encouraged her team to attend professional development training and made it accessible for them to do so by allocating money in the yearly budget. She also allowed her team members flexibility and expected them to accommodate each other's schedules for learning and other opportunities. She would often invite trainers within the organization to share what they had learned from educational workshops, and she encouraged team members to attend conferences or events to improve their practice.

Linda was transparent and openly communicated with her team about the budget limitations and education. Her team was very supportive of her, enjoyed the flexibility, and had a sense of belonging. After each conference, Linda expected the attendee to share some training takeaways with the team on their "leader-in-charge" days. These were pre-assigned leadership days when each team member served as leader and organizer of the department meeting.

She used the leaders in charge days to develop time-conscious, team-focused leaders who communicate effectively. Linda's leadership didn't allow for micromanagement.

Linda was reviewed as an engaging, respectful, and inclusive leader who values each team member. She promoted independence and trust within her department. Many people wanted to join Linda's department, and those there didn't want to leave. When team members are motivated to initiate and pursue learning opportunities, it improves their practice, retention, and communication and saves the company's money and reputation.

Becoming Leaders Who Promote Inclusion Excellence

I shared the Cinderella story as a metaphor for diversity, privilege, and inclusion and belonging in an equal opportunity environment. If your company were Cinderella's story, what kind of character would you be? Do some of your employees feel like Cinderella or her siblings? How would you find out? Our goal is to have fewer leaders like Cinderella's stepmother, who intentionally deny or discriminate against some of their employees by withholding opportunities for professional training or development.

Similarly, I hope your colleagues are not like Cinderella's siblings, who remain silent about her oppression and perpetuate discriminatory behavior because they are beneficiaries of privilege. We need mentors like the fairy godmother who not only believes in the employees but also recognizes and prepares them for opportunities. We definitely need prince-like leaders who are relentless in finding the right and deserving diverse talent despite their background or the time and effort required to find that talent.

Fortunately, we can choose to become the type of leaders we wish to have. Considering lack of training and employee development are cited as major issues affecting employee retention, it is important to have fairy godmother-like leaders who provide professional development opportunities through mentorship and sponsorship. We need leaders who see the best in employees and encourage them to seek opportunities. We need leaders who reach out to every team member until every diverse person gets a chance. Effective leaders recognize the challenges and ask questions to learn what their needs are. And once they learn, they use their privilege to offer resources to meet their teams' unique needs.

Cultural humility challenges us to become leaders who commit to inclusion excellence. Such leaders do not create different rules for different persons. Instead, they avoid unfair or discriminatory treatment and extend opportunities to all so they can bring out the best in everyone. With this approach, the by-products are improved communication, engagement, trust, positive and lasting relationships.

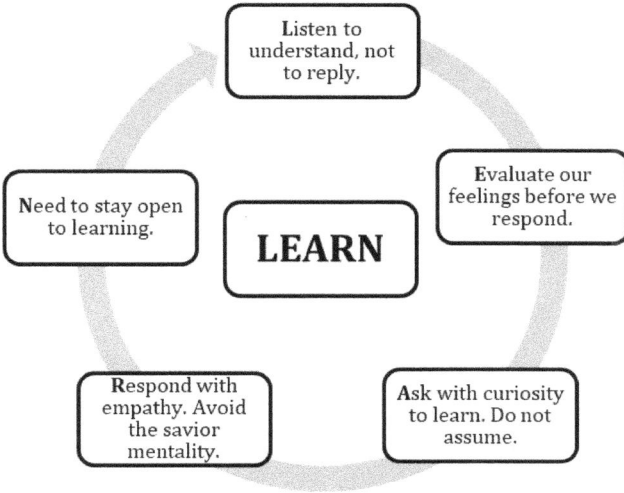

TAKEAWAYS

- Each individual we interact with needs some support. However, each individual doesn't need the same kind of support.
- Meeting people's needs gives them a sense of belonging.

CALL TO LEARN

- Utilize cultural humility to meet their unique needs equitably and inclusively.
- Ask your team to rate if you are a supportive or unsupportive leader.

MISTAKE #6

I will favor those who think like us and fit in our culture.

6

Lead with Consistency

People quit people, not companies. —John Maxwell

Unequal Treatment Is Not New

Remember the story where I was called a "colored girl?" That was my blessing in disguise because it led me to research, reflect, and be open-minded. When I talk about inconsistency and double standards from leadership, I think of the story of the runaway slaves. I imagine most people agree that slavery was wrong and evil, no matter who did it. The enslaved humans were inhumanely treated. The colonizers invented and innovated special tools and whips just for the slave's punishment. Enslaved people were put through verbal, physical, and psychological assault in the name of punishment. I have often wondered how mentally disturbed the colonizers were to treat other humans in such a cruel manner and be ok with it. I must say their mental wellness is questionable. There is one particular story that stands out for me when I think about double standards in leadership.

In 1640, three slaves, a Dutchman (Victor), Scotchman (James Gregory) and an African (John Punch) man, were brought before the court for sentencing because they ran away in an attempt to seek freedom. (I hope you notice the names. That is a whole other cultural name-stripping class.) Victor and James were sentenced to serve their master for one year and some change to make up for the loss that the master had sustained because of their absence. The entitlement by the colonizers and their legal system is appalling. John, "being a negro," was sentenced to serve his master or "his assigns" for the time of his natural life here or elsewhere. It is crazy how the system made sure that he was a prisoner and slave for the rest of his life, no matter where he was!

Today's Leadership Double Standards

Now, some of you may argue that this was a long time ago and that slavery ended. There are no slaves today. I agree that slavery is no longer legal. However, when unmanaged, biases lead to unfair and double standards.

Here is what one leader shared with me.

> *A few years ago, I was promoted as the first non-White person into a manager position in an organization. A few months later, the director, Karen, was excited to tell us that she was proud to have hired many leaders among them was one "diverse" leader. Karen invited us by hiring us. However, I don't think she or the department were ready to embrace us fully in our roles. You see, I had been with the company in different roles for over 10 years and never heard people question anyone promoted into a leadership role. However, when I was promoted, I heard people—some were leaders— wonder how I got there. I was the first non-White person to have that position. When I brought up what I was hearing to the company leadership, they sent out a company-wide memo explaining who we, new leaders, were and our qualifications. That was a quick fix, but the issue was deeper.*
>
> *One of the new managers, Sue, a White woman, had a*

difficult time transitioning and adjusting to her new leader-ship role. She said she was struggling because this job was too demanding and difficult for her. Karen was very support-ive with her and informed the team of the need to be patient and make accommodations for the new team members. She even offered Sue to take all the time she needed to train.

Would you believe that despite all the accommodation, one day, Sue neither showed up or called out work? Karen whose life lacks confidentiality, told the whole team that she and HR has reached out to Sue and offered her to re-turn to her previous role. Offering Sue her previous role was both kind and unusual gesture considering she had violated company policy. Albert Einstein once said, "Every-body is a genius. But if you judge a fish by its ability to climb a tree, it will live its whole life believing that it is stupid." It is impressive when leaders recognize and equitably meet the needs of their team. I have been surprised by how much people achieve when they feel supported.

Danni was the other "diverse" leader, a non-White woman, who was hired at the same time as Sue. Whenever Danni worked, Karen didn't directly communicate with her regardless of the situation. It was a very uncomfortable passive aggressive situation. When Danni made an error or mistake even if it was not clearly communicated, Karen literally yelled at her and threatened her with termination. On several occasions, I saw Danni in tears. Karen took her to HR for not learning quick enough and not completing her tasks. Unlike Sue, Danni was not offered more time to learn or her previous position. As a matter of fact, she was given a timeline to figure things out or be terminated. Most of my colleagues were aware of our department culture. Some were beneficiaries of Karen's niceness. I left for my mental well-being and self-preservation. When I brought up con-cerns and the need for a diversity committee as a safe space,

> *I was told that the committee is a good idea, but it was "not*
> *necessary right now due to budget and all the logistics."*

Cultures with unfair and cruel treatment are not only emotionally but also mentally exhausting. In such toxic cultures, those with power and privilege and their beneficiaries do not see a problem or the need to speak up. *Lack of inclusion and belonging are noticeable when they are missing.*

For my graduate studies, I focused on educator bias training and its effectiveness on learner achievement. Many studies show that unmanaged biases can create unfair and unpredictable environments. One study showed that teachers gave a lower grade on an assignment when it appeared to be authored by a Black student versus a White student. Another showed law firm professionals perceived memos presumed to be written by Black authors to have more grammatical errors than those perceived to be from White authors. The idea of creating different rules for different people stems from the expectation that people of the global majority are likely to make more mistakes than others. This goes back to the historical background of the USA and power and privilege imbalances.

When we fail to recognize inconsistencies, we continue to deny that there are double standards in how humans are treated. The pandemic exposed racial disparities in healthcare. The murder of George Floyd highlighted police brutality against African Americans that has been researched and documented by the American Public Health Association. The Great Resignation during the pandemic also let employers know that their employees do not feel a sense of belonging. The pandemic also showed that virtual learning was more beneficial for non-White students because they became more innovative as they were no longer being unfairly punished and sent to the principal's office while their peers were learning. They felt safe and achieved more at home.

The good news is we have an opportunity to be consistent and avoid double standards in our service. We start by acknowledging what is not just. Then setting fair and equitable standards and expectations of ourselves and those we serve. When we lead with cultural humility, we recognize and identify any biases we might have and use our privilege to consistently do good for the benefit of all.

Inconsistency in Leadership

Appreciating employees is important. When done correctly and consistently, it improves morale and promotes engagement. When inconsistent, employees notice and can become demoralized. When a leader shows favoritism for one team member while ignoring another, that behavior impacts the entire team culture. Leaders can definitely make or break their team. Here is what one workshop participant, Julie, said about her company:

Julie, described how a director decided to acknowledge their team at a monthly staff meeting. She would celebrate awards by giving shout-outs to anyone who got an award. She did it consistently until it was Julie's turn, who was named Teacher of the Year. The dean did not come to the ceremony to give the award. At the next faculty meeting, the award was not acknowledged by the dean until one of Julie's teaching colleagues stood up and congratulated her. Another colleague, Matt, had won and been celebrated for the same the month before. However, when Julie won, the director ignored her and didn't bring a cake as her usual ritual for the award recipient. The month Julie won, there was no cake, no shout-out or recognition of any sort. As a matter of fact, the monthly meeting was skipped altogether. At the next monthly meeting, another employee, Justine, had won and was being celebrated. The director brought cake as usual. At the celebration, Justine spoke up and mentioned Julie's great work and award from the previous month. The director tried to ignore it, but Justine insisted that Julie should be celebrated. Justine pointed out the double standards which were noticeable.

When one employee is treated favorably while another is treated unfavorably, people notice. We need to recognize what our leadership, expectations, and standards communicate to our teams or learners. We must show commitment to all especially the marginalized employees so we can improve relationships and promote engagement.

Another workshop participant, Pete, shared his observations about his nursing program:

> At the hospital, most of our nursing assistants are also student nurses. There are countable nurses of color in our department. Some White nurses mentor the White nursing assistants who are students and share many encouraging words with them. They say things like, "Feel free to study once you have checked on all your patients. I know nursing school is hard." They invite them to observe various procedures and even supervise their learning opportunities. Whenever these students are late, these employees are quick to forgive them by saying, "Oh, let's give them a few minutes. They will be here. We were students once. Let's be patient." On the other hand, the students of color do not get the same treatment. If they were seen with their study materials at work, they would be written up for studying. They would not be invited to see any special procedures or assist in any activity for learning purposes. If they were late, they would be punished and warned for being late. One was told, "You must choose between going to school or coming to work. You decide which one is a priority."

Eleanor, another workshop participant and student, added:

It was our first day of class, and the professor asked us to introduce ourselves as we collected our syllabus and supplies from her. There were five students of color out of 40 students. And yes, I counted us. Every time a White student approached the professor, who was sitting in front of the class, she smiled, looked up at them, welcomed them to her class, and offered herself if they needed anything. When a Black student approached her, she didn't even look up. She continued looking at her books on her desk and handed them their items without smiling. When I approached her, she asked me how many times I had attempted to get into this program. I told her this was my first time. She then looked at me and said that I must have gotten lucky but that luck is not going to get me far, especially not with a C. Mind you, I am an A student, so I have no idea who she was confusing me for. I was shocked. I noticed she did not smile, not even to one student of color. Let us just say, this professor made me work triple hard to get my A. Her interaction with Black and White students was like night and day!

Consistency Sets Clear and Inclusive Expectations

Have you seen or experienced such situations as those described above? These are real-life stories that are examples of inconsistent leadership. Effective leadership is consistent, predictable, and doesn't create different rules for different people. Every day we have an opportunity to reflect on how we treat, highlight or give feedback to our teams. Our leadership affects our team or clients positively or negatively.

Leadership is about relationships. By definition, we influence people every day. It is part of the job. It doesn't matter whether influencing is part of our profession or not; it is our responsibility, as we affect those we serve through teaching, leading, coaching, mentoring, and every other way we interact with them. It is essential to operate from a place of fairness. Effective leadership sets standards and clear expectations for everyone. It doesn't mean we tolerate tardiness or overlook mistakes from people. It just means that to be inclusive we must treat everyone fairly and consistently.

It is essential to be aware of our actions, interactions, and our power imbalance. When we treat everyone fairly, and communicate clearly, people are aware of that expectation. When we fall short of that expectation, people definitely notice the unfairness, especially those to whom it is directed. Leading with cultural humility fosters the just and fair expectations from and for us and our teams.

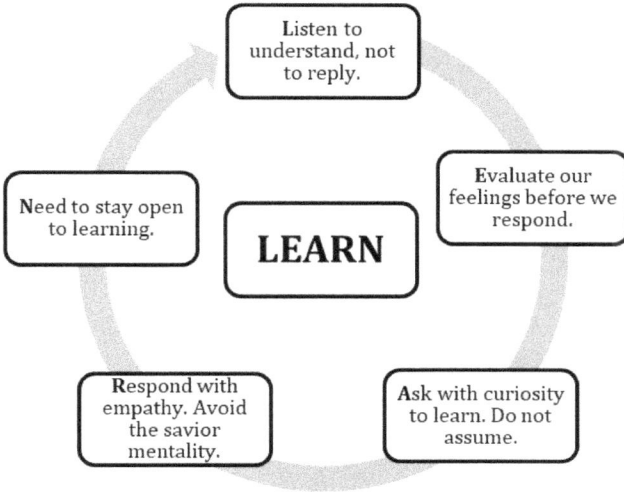

TAKEAWAYS

- Lack of inclusion and belonging are noticeable when they are missing.
- Inclusive leadership avoids double standards and practices fairness to everyone.

CALL TO LEARN

- Do you notice any inconsistencies in serving your team?
- Assess if your team can safely and comfortably share their honest feedback with you.

MISTAKE #7

*I have good intentions
and that is all that
matters.*

7

Good Intention ≠ Good Impact

One doesn't have to operate with great malice to do great harm.
The absence of empathy and understanding are sufficient. In fact, a
man convinced of his virtue even in the midst of his vice is the
worst kind of man.—Charles M. Blow

How Can I Show Appreciation?

S tudies show that appreciating your team or staff promotes engagement, retention, and productivity. Most good leaders have sincere intentions to appreciate their teams. They agree that expressing gratitude and showing it is a wonderful way to acknowledge your team. But while appreciating your team is a great way to show your gratitude and motivate them, unintentional efforts can lead to a feeling of exclusion, the opposite of the goal of inclusion in a diverse team. Most companies have networking events set up to increase employee engagement and connection.

At a workshop training, this is what some participants had to say about happy hour, a common well-intentioned networking event:

- For personal reasons, I don't drink alcohol. Do we have to meet over liquor? I am sure there are many places we can meet comfortably.
- One time, I ordered cranberry juice. Boy, was I ever made fun of! All the guys at my table teased that I was drinking the ladies' drink. Trying to get through that evening was mentally exhausting.
- As a recovering alcoholic, I avoid happy hour events because I get anxious. I really do not want to be near any of that.
- I wish events could have classier non-alcoholic selections. There aren't many options to choose from.

As common and well-intended an event happy hour is, be aware that your good intentions may end up creating anxiety and mental exhaustion. A cultural humility approach means asking one more question. Sometimes a few minutes of a simple survey or a few seconds of selecting a box is all it takes to be aware of people's needs. Inviting diverse people is a start. Defaulting to the majority's norm often excludes them. Therefore, intentional gestures of care and conscientiousness, no matter how small, cultivate cultures of belonging.

Instead of assuming that everyone likes gifts, the same gifts, or has a similar gift preference, ask one more question. As a leader, you can ask your team if they are ok with receiving gifts or company parties. If they do, find out their preference. If not, inquire from them how they would show appreciation. You can send out an anonymous survey to collect data to learn more about your team and increase engagement. Asking questions in a safe way promotes engagement. Listening with empathy to learn can make everyone feel seen. As Maya Angelou once said, "I've learned that people will forget what you said, people will forget what you did, but people will never forget how you made them feel." By meeting your team's unique needs and preferences, you make them feel, seen, and valued. Often, people with privilege dismiss DEI work as being all about feelings. While it is about feelings, it is also about being cost-effective and avoiding costly mistakes.

That One Further Question

Recently, I read a story with the headline, "US man wins $450k lawsuit after unwanted office birthday party." In this story, *an employee won a settlement of hundreds of thousands of dollars after he sued a company that had violated him. As a sign of employee recognition and appreciation, the company had a cultural norm of throwing birthday parties for their employees. According to the article, the employee had declined the party, yet his leader insisted on having one for him. The leader gave him a lecture and told him that not having the party would inconvenience the team and that it was a sign of not being a team player and insubordination. This is a classic reflection of when leaders use their power and privilege to do as they please and often perpetuate oppression against a single employee. The story further explains that the employee had a history of panic attacks, and this affected his mental health. However, despite the lawsuit and settlement, the company is adamant about blaming the victim, which caused more harm and suffering to the victim. The employee did everything he could to advocate for himself. They did not listen to him. They ignored him. And then made themselves out to be his victims by promoting what is important to the company and the majority of the team. By refusing to acknowledge their wrongdoing, the organization perpetuates a culture where they not only failed at being just to their employee but also caused him harm. This clearly reflects on the company's toxic culture and reputation.*

Biases and stereotypes lead to poor communication, offensive behavior, discrimination, or prejudices. Simply put, they are destructive because they cause suffering. Now that we know that we all have biases and studies show that unmanaged biases, even from well-intentioned leaders, create a negative impact, we need to focus on managing our biases to appropriately serve or lead others. Managing biases improves communication, saves time and, as we have seen, millions of dollars by asking just one more question. It also improves communication and builds lasting relationships.

Most anyone who has gone through educational or professional training has been taught to apply cultural competence to manage biases. Even though our educational and professional training emphasizes cultural competence, anthropological research recommends utilizing cultural humility instead of competence because one cannot ostensibly be competent in another's culture. The notion of competence is grounded in a Western perspective, where one group is viewed as superior to others, and individuals' needs are assumed as a group's needs. For example, while preparing for a clinical assignment in nursing school, we had to learn about the culture of the patients we might care for and review some of their background data. We "learned," for example, that most people of Asian descent prefer warm water. Therefore, as a culturally competent nurse caring for a patient of Asian descent, out of good intent, it was expected that I bring them warm water when they asked for water. Over the years, I have realized that some Asian patients do not like warm water. Some prefer room temperature, cold, or ice water, while others do not like water at all.

Good Intent Doesn't Equal Good Impact

> *Nurse Mora had thoroughly read the patient's chart to gain insight into his needs and how his cultural practices might affect his care. And, citing cultural competence, she surmised that since her patient was from a certain town in Minnesota and belonged to a particular race, he must be Lutheran. This is because most people from that city are Lutheran. In trying to support the family and let the daughter spend time with her father, Nurse Mora went ahead and paged the chaplain line and requested a Lutheran minister. A few moments later, the chaplain arrived, and she showed him to the patient's room. The patient's daughter, who had been holding her father's hand while waiting, was excited to see the two return so promptly. However, she was not sure why a Lutheran minister was standing at her father's bedside.*
>
> *The daughter looked disappointed as she told Nurse Mora and the chaplain that her father didn't need a Lutheran minister. Instead, he needed a rabbi. The nurse apologized profusely to her patient, the daughter, and the chaplain. The chaplain left the room to page for a rabbi. As Nurse Mora tearfully recounted the story to our team, we all realized that good intent doesn't equal good impact. If only she had stopped to ask the patient's daughter what her father's preference was, she could have avoided the disappointment and saved time and resources. There would have been a happy family whose needs were met by a happy nurse. All it took was asking one more question.*

By utilizing a cultural humility approach, we can ask one more question to find out what the preference actually is, not what we assume it to be. This will avoid making inaccurate assumptions and wasting time and offer accurate resources that meet the unique clients' needs.

As leaders, we need to know that it is important not merely to focus on what we were taught or may already know but on what we don't know about the student, client, patient, colleague, or customer standing or sitting in front of us. This can only happen through self-reflection about what we are used to, what we know, our culture and experiences, and then realizing the limitation of our knowledge of others. We should then ask one more question with curiosity and listen with empathy to learn. By normalizing not knowing everything, our expert knowledge will not interfere or create a wall that blocks what we are about to learn. When we listen with empathy, we will hear the person or message, not because we are doing them a favor, but because their experience needs to be heard and valued. This is how we build trust so we can offer solutions, realizing that people are unique. They are not projects to be completed or objects to be fixed but people who *need to be understood.*

The Million-Dollar Question

There was a company that needed to fill a secretarial role that required some traveling. The applicant they hired said that she was willing and able to travel, as was part of the job requirement, and she made human resources aware that she was disabled and had some limitations. One day, while the secretary and her boss were attending an event, an emergency situation forced her boss to park a long distance away from the venue. Her boss sped ahead of her, walking briskly toward the venue and imploring her to keep up. But due to her disability and the location of the parking spot, the secretary was unable to make it to the venue before the doors closed. She missed the important event. Once she returned to the office, her boss yelled at her and told her that her lateness would not be tolerated next time.

She tried to explain to the boss that she had a medical con-
dition that caused her to have a disability. As a matter of
fact, she had communicated to human resources upon hire
that she had one leg amputated years ago due to an illness.
Unfortunately, she was not accommodated. Instead, she got
yelled at and considered incompetent. It is not surprising
that she quit the job and sued her boss. The secretary had
clearly explained her disability to human resources, who
hired her because she was qualified for the job. Her disabil-
ity was clearly discussed with the hiring body.

I have often wondered if HR had communicated this special accommodation with her boss. The boss could have avoided and prevented the lawsuit had he stopped, controlled his emotions, and asked one more question to understand why this employee was late. The mistake ended up costing the company over a million dollars.

A mentor once told me that people sue not because they like to but because they do not feel listened to. This story is a great reminder that leadership is about relationships, building rapport and learning about the people we cross paths with every day. In this situation, the time wasted, the emotional stress caused, the turnover cost, and millions in lawsuits would have been saved with one simple cultural humility approach: Stop, reflect, and ask one more question to learn so we can achieve a positive outcome. This is a great reminder that when we miss focusing on the inclusion of diversity, we create negative outcomes.

Paying Attention to the Answers

Considering that all human beings consciously and unconsciously store experiences in their long-term memories, let us recognize that we have biases and utilize cultural humility to manage them instead of suppressing them. Effective leaders must ask questions, engage in conversations that challenge stereotypes, and develop meaningful relationships. Such leaders are self-aware when interacting with those from marginalized or minoritized groups and backgrounds. They work to improve their listening skills and pay attention to their client's or team's tiniest and deepest detail to learn more about their backgrounds, cultures, and beliefs. Paying attention helps leaders provide their followers with the most appropriate and adequate resources to produce the best outcomes. When we utilize cultural humility, we ask one more question, improving communication, relationships, eliminating stereotypes, decreasing turnover, saving money, and leading to excellent outcomes.

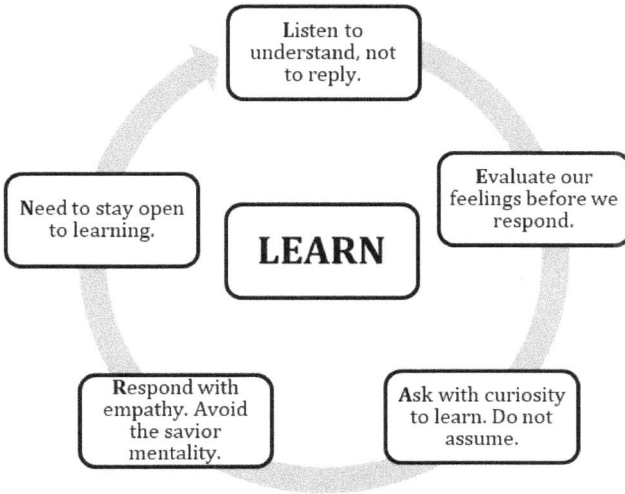

TAKEAWAYS

- Good intent does not always lead to good impact.
- By asking one more question, you focus on impact and avoid making assumptions.

CALL TO LEARN

- Ask people for their preferences.
- Listen to learn and understand, not to reply.

MISTAKE #8

I am the expert.
I know everything.

PRACTICE

8

Normalize Not Knowing Everything

*It is impossible for a (hu)man to learn what
he thinks he already knows.*—Epictetus

Not Knowing is OK If We Are Willing to Learn

We live in a society that celebrates and praises experts. Our cultures see experts as intelligent, competent, and knowledgeable. Those who say they do not know or may not know something risk being looked down upon as incompetent. This has driven many people to act as if they know everything, despite being uncertain, because they don't want to be seen as stupid or incompetent. After all, we are taught that we should fake it until we make it.

Unfortunately, when it comes to people and relationships, most people never make it *because they faked it*. Cultural humility challenges us to normalize not knowing everything by asking questions with curiosity, listening with empathy to understand, and staying open to learning. This approach allows us to be vulnerable and authentic. It gives one permission to say, "Even though I know a lot, I don't know everything. So, please show me, tell me, or teach me." It reminds us that we need to listen and learn from others despite their age, background, position, abilities, or experience.

Even though most of us grew up hearing that there is no stupid question and that the only stupid question is the one not asked, we still struggle to embrace the idea that asking questions or saying, "I do not know, but let me find out" is okay. When leaders normalize not knowing everything, they display their authenticity and vulnerability by asking to learn or for help from someone who looks up to them for direction and leadership. This inspires, challenges, and invites their teams to do the same. More than that, normalizing not knowing everything helps your staff feel unafraid to ask "out of place" questions or admit when they don't know something. It permits them to ask questions to avoid making mistakes or preventable errors. It provides opportunities to create conversations, promote engagement, prevent errors, save time, and increase trust, building lasting relationships.

We have been trained to believe that we appear stupid or incompetent when we say that we don't know. But it can be dangerous if we pretend to know something we don't. Doing so can make the wrong decision that causes harm or suffering. It can waste resources that could be saved and utilized elsewhere. It can take time to correct a preventable error, and sometimes we do not get another opportunity to fix the mistake or bring back a life lost.

Humility is Not Humiliation

A few years ago, I taught at a local community public health forum. Most attendees were excited to share their experiences and learn more about cultural humility. They were especially intrigued by the fact that cultural humility challenges leaders to acknowledge the limitations of what they may or may not know about their clients and recognize their power and how that may affect those they are serving. Here is what one workshop attendee, Zuri, had to say about her experience of her last doctor's visit:

One time, I went to the doctor for my blood pressure check-up. I know he is qualified to be a doctor because he went to school for a long time. But he didn't listen to me. When I told him that a certain medication, he had prescribed for me, made me feel worse when I took it, can you believe this man dismissed my concerns? He told me I was lucky to have insurance to afford such an amazing medication that works for many people! After that visit, I fired that doctor and quit that medication. I never went back to him or the clinic. Last year, when I was so sick, I just went to the ER.

From this experience, Zuri went to the doctor because she saw him as an expert. However, not listening to her concerns drove Zuri away and gave her a reason not to trust him. She ended up using an expensive resource, the emergency room, for cost-effective preventative care. Maybe you have heard similar stories where leaders don't listen to their patients, teams, or students and flash their expert credentials or title at every instance of being challenged. When we do this, we are trying to communicate:

- I know more than you and nothing you think or say is meaningful.
- I went to school for a long time to earn my credentials. Do not question my authority.
- We have always done it this way. Don't question our work.

While I agree that we need experts and that it takes many years of education to get qualified, *humility* is not *humiliation*. Humility is not discrediting. Pausing to listen to your followers, acknowledging that you do not know everything, and then asking to learn is essential in building trust in leadership. It is essential to involve those you are trying to impact. Anyone can be a leader. But not everyone is an effective leader. Effective inclusive leaders normalize not knowing everything by listening to their clients and offering unique solutions that meet their individual needs. Studies show that patients will trust a provider who listens to them. They will not take or follow a prescribed or recommended regimen from a provider they do not trust. Inclusion fosters trust.

Humility Fosters Trust in Our Expertise

While I was working as a new leader supervising staff and assigning patient care to nurses, my manager walked up to my desk and urgently asked to speak with me. My heart sank as I followed her to her office, afraid that I may have done something wrong. The manager immediately pointed to some articles on her desk and asked me, "What is a STEMI or NSTEMI?" I told her what these abbreviations stood for and their meaning. She thanked me for the information and explained that she had a deadline to meet as she was preparing for our hospital's annual evaluation by the accrediting body. Initially, I thought she was just quizzing me to determine my knowledge base as a new leader. However, I later found out that she genuinely appreciated the answers. She was afraid to use the acronyms incorrectly, worried that someone would argue that she should not be a manager if she didn't know what those abbreviations meant or where to find the information. She confessed she felt mentally and physically exhausted from dealing with a critically sick child and an ailing parent. Plus, she had been working all week, and her mind, she described, "had completely gone blank." The next time I worked, she left me a thank-you note and a whole tiramisu cake. This experience taught me it is a good thing to acknowledge that we do not know everything as long as we ask to learn, save time, and avoid mistakes. It also showed me that a great leader does not know everything but is willing to learn from and trust their team.

Do Not Assume. Ask Instead.

When we lack cultural humility, we stereotype others by making inaccurate assumptions and conclusions. Equitable and inclusive practices take work. This means we recognize our power and privilege and use it for good. It means we notice differences and assume nothing. It also means we invite others into conversation, then listen with empathy, not to reply but to identify solutions to their needs. The following story is about a leader who recognized his power and privilege and used empathy to do good:

A CEO was making rounds in different departments in his company. He walked into one department and saw one of his employees seemingly asleep on her desk. He walked close to her and woke her up. She was startled and jumped up from her sleep. Right away, she knew she was in trouble and could be terminated because sleeping during work was against company policy. The boss asked if she was ok and kept on with his making rounds.

Later that day, she received an email from the boss asking her to come to his office. Her stomach sank. She knew she was going to lose her job. She was so afraid that she could not stop crying. Once she got into the boss's office, he started the conversation by sharing that he understands people get tired for many reasons. He shared that he remembers being exhausted from caring for his sick father. He said that it was very difficult, and he remembers not many people were supportive of him then.

Crying, the employee empathized with her boss and felt safe to explain herself. She said that she, too, had a sick, elderly parent and a child who had been unwell recently. She had been awake all night. She begged the boss not to fire her because she was the sole breadwinner as her husband had recently been laid off. She told her boss she was sorry and willing to do anything not to lose her job. The boss listened.

After a few moments, he picked up the phone and called HR. The employee thought this call was to get her fired. The boss turned and asked the employee how much time she would need to focus on her family before returning to work. He then authorized HR to give the employee the necessary time off so she could care for her family.

This leader could have assumed the employee was on drugs or had been up late partying the night before. He could have chosen to follow the company policy to terminate the team member. However, he chose to ask one more question to learn what was happening. He used his power and privilege to do good. This situation also gave HR a great opportunity to focus on resourcing the humans within the company. The employee remained with the company for 16 years. Leading with empathy not only promotes retention and employee satisfaction but also avoids losing good employees. If employees' needs are noted and addressed, the employer can save millions of dollars in turnover or training costs. Indeed, we can do this even when it seems like the company policies are stating something else entirely. Even if we didn't experience support in our past, we can still practice empathy and make others feel safe, supported and secure.

Saying We Don't Know but Being Willing to Learn

The solution is to normalize not knowing, ask questions with curiosity to learn, listen with empathy to understand, and stay open to learning. This cultural humility practice allows leaders to recognize that when we neglect to ask questions and act as if we know it all, we miss out on challenging assumptions and stereotypes and learning new ways to think about the world around us. We unintentionally make biased decisions that negatively affect those we serve or cause suffering to others. As leaders, we are challenged to become learn-it-alls instead of know-it-alls. We need leaders who will truly listen, be unafraid of challenging exclusive policies, and recognize the power that comes with their position and titles, so they can invite and model for their team how to be vulnerable and authentic lifelong learners.

Normalize Not Knowing Everything to Create Cultures of Belonging

Humans, across the board, can be harsh toward people who are different than the societal "norm," whatever that may be, including those who are more intelligent or ambitious than average. Consider how different groups perceive each other. Consider stereotypical assumptions about certain people. For example, some people believe African Americans are lazy, Africans are primitive and Asians are super smart especially in the sciences. Where do such biases come from? Do you see how such believes can deny or extend opportunities unfairly? To be considered an expert, indeed, a leader in a certain field or profession, takes many years of effort.

My hope is we will utilize cultural humility so we can ask one more question to learn about individuals as unique not assume based on the group they are a part of. I hope we will come to respect what is exceptional in others, whether it is something we are born with or is the result of the hard work and time it takes to become an expert. I hope that as leaders, we recognize our expertise, which gives us power and privilege, and use it to help others. Cultural humility challenges us to question our assumptions and be flexible enough to be open to learning new ideas and strategies, even from those we don't consider experts.

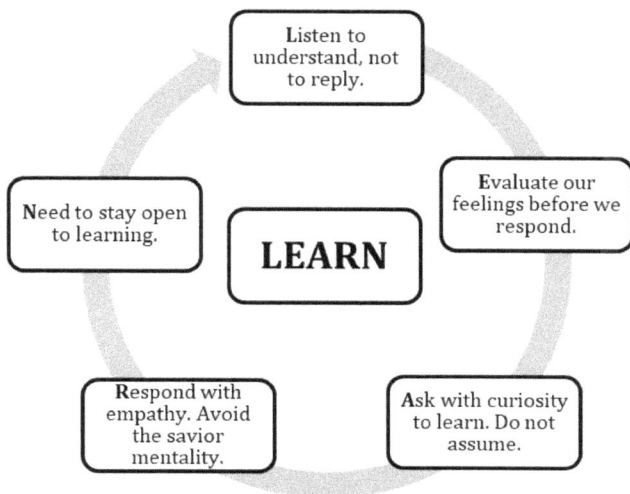

TAKEAWAYS

- Humility is not humiliation: we can learn from anyone.
- When we normalize not knowing everything, we build trust and become lifelong learners.

CALL TO LEARN

- Question some of your assumptions.
- Practice asking one more question so you can become a learn-it-all instead of a know-it-all.

MISTAKE #9

I am afraid of saying the wrong thing.

9

Don't Be Afraid to Say the "Wrong" Thing

Courage is the most important of all the virtues, because without courage, you can't practice any other virtue consistently. —Maya Angelou

Safe to Grow and Adapt

Over the years, I have reflected on my cultural background, beliefs, and attitudes towards different things, and I realize that I don't do or say some things I used to anymore. Some of my views have changed because I now have new information, insights, or experiences. Some of the assumptions and conclusions I made were incorrect. I have grown. What else has changed? Times have changed; we now have more information and we are now exposed to different cultures. This is why we leaders must be lifelong learners who must adapt—because cultures evolve and information changes. These shifts affect our attitudes, perceptions, and beliefs. With the current demographic changes, global connections, and technological advancements, I hope we can stay open to learning while we cultivate cultures for our followers to not only belong but also adapt. We must create environments where we encourage our teams to listen and feel free to speak up. As Michael Jordan once said, "I can accept failure, but I cannot accept not trying." We must try. Our teams, clients, and students need a supportive space to take risks and make mistakes. They need a brave environment to learn and sincerely speak their minds, and that example begins with us. It starts with accountability and ownership when we make mistakes and communicating with transparency to correct them and learn.

Correcting Our Gaffes

In 2021, I attended a virtual conference for diversity, equity, and inclusion experts. In one of many learning activities in break-out rooms, my group received instructions that we were to engage each other. Then we would select one individual to summarize our conversation in one minute for the entire group. After engaging in robust discussions for a few minutes, the coordinator reconvened everyone to share their summaries. Our group chose José to share our ideas. When it was his turn to speak, José was quiet for a few seconds, to which the coordinator reminded him, "You are unmuted, speak on and out." A few more seconds went by before José started to speak. In great detail, he explained exactly what we discussed. He then took a few more seconds to say, "My name is José. I am an executive at [. . .]. I am a certified interpreter. I have a stutter, and I speak six languages fluently." Everyone was in awe, then clapping for José took a few more seconds. The conference coordinator was embarrassed but also inspired. She apologized for assuming that everyone needed only one minute and that she was impatient when José did not meet the set time expectations. She then apologized for thinking that José was muted or technologically challenged. The coordinator apologized for not being equitable in accommodating everyone.

Finally, she said that she hoped everyone learned as much as she learned from this experience. She then announced that if there was anyone who needed more time to express themselves, they were allowed to do so. She immediately corrected her behavior with actions.

Perhaps most of us have had similar experiences. Since the COVID-19 pandemic, we have had to adapt to a virtual world at breakneck speed. Running meetings virtually, conducting interviews over Zoom, assigning students to break-out sessions, all with the assumption that every person is aware of (and tech-savvy enough) to meet the set expectations. Considering the differences in age, ability, expertise, internet availability and accessibility, and the amount of time it takes one to communicate, clearly equity should be at the forefront. In the case mentioned above, equality wasn't an effective way to lead. An equitable approach would have allowed José the time and space to effectively communicate. We are reminded that no matter how much expertise we have in a subject or how prepared we may think we are, any person can make a mistake. As Maya Angelou said, "Courage is the most important of all the virtues, because without courage you can't practice any other virtue consistently. You can practice any virtue erratically, but nothing consistently without courage." Leaders must learn to apologize, correct the mistake, and use it as a learning opportunity to prevent a repeat of the same in the future. The coordinator's response was definitely an exhibition of courage.

The Cost of Preventable Mistakes

When people are not equipped with resources to manage their biases, they end up making costly mistakes. A few years ago, a bank teller called the police on a customer attempting to deposit a large amount of money. In her mind and experience, even though she had served many customers who deposited large amounts, the teller was afraid that the customer may not have legally acquired such a large sum of money. The police arrived and surprised the customer when they told him they were called to investigate him. Upon identifying the customer, they realized he was a businessman depositing money he had legally earned for his company. Only the teller knows what was going through her mind to cause her to fear. She did explain that, though many customers had deposited such large amounts, she felt that the customer didn't fit the profile of having such a large amount of money. It is said that the teller sought a second opinion from her supervisor before calling the police. Her supervisor confirmed the teller's fears by allowing the decision to call the police.

How Could Cultural Humility Prevent This Outcome?

Unmanaged biases, even well-intentioned, cause harm. If the teller had applied cultural humility, she could have stopped and asked one more question about her thinking. This would have interrupted her automatic and prejudiced reaction by questioning her fearful belief. The cultural humility approach would have challenged the supervisor to address the teller's concerns and instead strike a conversation with the customer out of curiosity. The teller and her supervisor would have listened with empathy to recognize their unfounded assumptions. Instead, the customer sued the bank and received millions in the settlement.

This incident also led to many wasted resources. The police could have been in much-needed areas solving real crimes. Considering the named bank is a chain business, the company was affected nationwide as it lost customers, received bad press, and had to invest in training the employees on implicit bias. Acknowledging your bias, interrupting your thoughts, and asking questions to learn could have saved all these resources and led to positive outcomes and remarkable customer experiences. Clearly, this was a preventable but costly mistake and apology.

Effective Leaders Apologize

Dr. Jan, a doctor and community leader, was tasked with leading a diverse community. In the spirit of leadership and to improve community engagement and unity, she planned several community gatherings. She decided to start with the African American community to which she belonged. She reserved the event date, venue, catering, and invited speakers. She then sent out flyers to invite all members of the community. She wanted to lead by example by making sure everyone felt comfortable. Then, just two nights before the event, she got a call from a community member in the middle of the night. The caller asked her if she was aware that the date she had chosen to celebrate the African American community was a Jewish holiday. Shocked, Dr. Jan told the caller that she was not aware. The caller asked her to look at the city's calendar. Sure enough, there was a word on the calendar in a language she didn't recognize. Dr. Jan apologized to the caller, thanked her, and told her she would correct the mistake. The next day, she woke up early and sent an email to her team to apologize and share the lesson learned. Even though this had taken months of planning, Dr. Jan called all her speakers, vendors, and community leaders and explained what she had learned in all transparency. In the words of Winston Churchill, "Courage is what it takes to stand up and speak; courage is also what it takes to sit down and listen." Everyone, without resistance, thanked her and decided to join the Jewish community to celebrate and learn more about their holiday. She rescheduled the

> *African American event to another date. The Jewish community was very appreciative of that gesture.*

Douglas MacArthur stated that a leader does "not set out to be a leader, but becomes one by the equality of his actions and the integrity of his intent." Great leadership doesn't mean we do what's easy or only listen to those we like. It means we do the uncomfortable work: listen to everyone—even those we do not like. We stand up and do what's right even when it feels too far to turn back or it requires us to stand alone. Great leaders see a learning opportunity when they make a mistake, no matter how many steps they have to take or how many people they must talk to. They know to own the responsibility to apologize and learn from their mistakes.

When we take responsibility for our actions, we give our followers permission to be unafraid to make mistakes and be transparent in learning. Sometimes, our followers may say or do the wrong thing. We are still responsible for owning the missteps, training, providing our teams with resources to make the right decisions, and then holding them accountable after appropriately training them. When your employees are empowered with an environment to learn, they become transparent in communicating their shortcomings and looking to grow. Following their leader's example, they also become unafraid of saying or doing the wrong thing or making a mistake. We need leaders who set out to influence for good by cultivating cultures or environments where the followers can grow and develop, thrive and change rather than be afraid of losing their jobs or being punished.

What is the Missing Piece?

My daughter, Makayla, loves sorting, organizing and solving puzzles. She is *thorough*. When she is set to put together a puzzle, she will work until she finds *all* the missing pieces. I have watched her put a piece upside down, sideways, or wrong side up, and when it doesn't fit, she puts it away and tries a different piece. She stays at it until she finds the right one. She persists until she succeeds. Once she solves the puzzle, the whole image makes sense. She is so excited! Her excitement is contagious.

The leadership lesson here is that mistakes are like missing puzzle pieces. Once we own mistakes—take accountability—we should be determined to correct them. We should keep trying to find the correct strategy until we effectively solve a problem. For example, if we want to correct mistakes to improve our relationships, we must practice effective communication by learning and using inclusive language and keep trying until we get it right. It will all come together as long as we keep looking for the right pieces (knowing the practices) and placing them in the missing spots (implementing through action) to correct our behavior. Our goal is to complete the puzzle, that is, to become inclusive leaders who leave people feeling seen, heard, and valued.

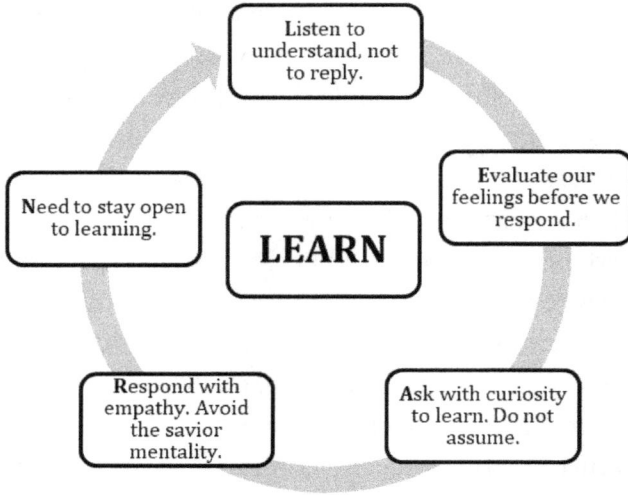

TAKEAWAYS

- An apology is a sign of growth and effective leadership.
- A sincere apology has three parts. Taking responsibility for the mistake, having a willingness to correct the mistake, and correcting the mistake. This shows courage, learning and growth.

PRACTICE (Giving A Sincere Apology)

If you or your employees make a mistake, here is how to give a sincere apology:

- Take responsibility. Say, for example, "I apologize for the mistake that has been made."
- Name the mistake made and communicate clearly.
- Mention that the mistake was done, but stress that you are willing to learn and correct the mistake.
- Ask "What can I do to help?" in your plan for correction.
- Offer help following the suggestion.

MISTAKE #10

Why change when we have always done it this way?

PRACTICE

10

Notice, Demystify, Evolve

We can knowingly strive to be an antiracist. Like fighting an addiction, being an antiracist requires persistent self-awareness, constant self-criticism, and regular self-examination.—Ibram X. Kendi

Showing Up

S ince the murder of George Floyd in 2020 by a Minneapolis police officer, leaders and companies are seeing the world more clearly and intentionally spending millions in attempting to create inclusive cultures. Most leaders are working towards becoming inclusive and checking on their teams for feedback to determine if their companies are providing a sense of belonging. It is our job, as leaders, to cultivate a culture of belonging for the people we serve by showing up in our work environment and demonstrating to the marginalized, minoritized, underprivileged, underrepresented and underserved that we will take the lead and have their backs. It is our responsibility to welcome them by creating safe and supportive environments.

LEADING WITH CULTURAL HUMILITY

Focus on Adding to the Culture Instead of "Culture-Fit"

For years, we have heard about a good "culture-fit" when it comes to recruiting or hiring. This simply means that an employee or potential candidate has beliefs, values, and behaviors that align with the potential employer. The intent was good. However, those with diverse views, opinions, ideas, and behaviors are often disqualified or deselected, and as a result the company's culture has little diversity. To be productive and efficient, we don't have to be the same or like the same things. The greatest skill that will promote inclusion is realizing that I am not you and you are not me. Leaders should instead focus on recruiting from diverse cultures. Once we hire people from marginalized or minoritized backgrounds, we must embrace their differences and encourage authenticity so these new members can add to the company culture and not just "fit."

Give A Second Chance Instead of Disqualifying on A First Impression

There is an old saying that a first impression is everything. This is all good until people realize that all people do not have the same background or circumstances. When invited for an interview, most people prepare. However, due to illnesses or various medical conditions, some people become anxious, affecting how they interact at that first meeting. To be inclusive, we must take into account different situations and personalities. Then consider extending grace to everyone. This is also true of a great candidate who is late for an appointment due to a lack of transportation or a sick child. While at it, let us revisit our assumptions about a candidate's appearance. What is a "professional look?" I argue that a professional look is not universal or a one size fits all.

When I went through nursing school, everyone was expected to wear their hair straight back. TV reporters and dancers were made to relax their hair using chemicals to smooth it and wear it straight back. This is a standard set by a White aesthetic value system. Having curly or kinky hair was not considered professional, and this translated to missed opportunities or deselection of Black candidates. The good news is that some of these discriminatory and outdated practices are being removed. For example, the recently passed Crown Act Bill allows Black people to wear their hair in its natural state. Now companies cannot deselect candidates they consider to appear "unprofessional." Inclusion is an active process and a work in progress.

Are Your Policies Outdated or Exclusive?

Recently, a friend lost her uncle, the man who raised her, and she needed to make a long trip from the United States to India for his funeral. Most equal opportunity employers give three days of paid funeral leave. If someone needs more time for a non-qualifying family member or extended family, like in my friend's case, a manager has to determine if that is possible based on their budget. Such policies are exclusive and discriminatory. There is no argument that most organizations are equal-opportunity employers. However, considering demographic changes and the ever-changing definition of family, some company policies are outdated and only serve some employees. These policies need to be addressed and reviewed so they can serve all employees.

Three days might be acceptable for someone who comes from the same local community as the employer, but for people who have moved for their work or even immigrated from abroad, it is an insufficient amount of time (especially in this day and age) to make a trip and return. When my father and grandmother passed away, I was fortunate to have an amazing manager who empa-

LEADING WITH CULTURAL HUMILITY

thized with me and saw my humanity as I grieved my losses and I needed to travel to Africa for the funerals. Now that we have sophisticated digital technologies, it should not be unreasonable for employers to give actual time off and also to permit remote work to support long-distance travel when circumstances require it. This is a win-win for everyone: a grieving employee can pay her respects and the company still has a productive employee.

Everyone Can Learn and Adapt

We have heard of the saying, "You cannot teach an old dog new tricks or an old dog cannot learn new tricks." I argue that these are myths. We miss growth and development opportunities when we assume that an old dog cannot learn new tricks. If in doubt, the pandemic showed us that everyone can learn and is capable of adapting. Instead of assuming that some people are too stuck in their ways to learn, leaders should champion change and lead by adapting to change to give followers an opportunity to learn. We are challenged to acknowledge that we might be the "old dogs" who may need to adapt to a new growth mindset. We should remember that learning is not a destination but a process. The pandemic taught us that the world can function virtually and make big shifts when it has to. We learned that people can adapt successfully, even in a crisis. Effective inclusive leaders embrace learning and adapting inclusive practices to make everyone feel safe, secure, and supported. For example, they make meetings less techy to prevent ageism.

Remember, for our purposes, we can take this further to the understanding that in the context of cultural humility work, we can all LEARN.

Authorize and Create Inclusive Spaces

Diversity thrives in cultures of belonging. Let us use our privilege to do good by authorizing inclusive practices in our organizations. There are many ways to create inclusive spaces. Here are some examples:

Marginalization by	Create Inclusive Spaces
Religion	Build a prayer room for people with different religious practices.
Sex	Designate a childcare center.
	Build lactation or nursing rooms.
Sexual Orientation	Construct or assign all-person restrooms.
Ability	Build a ramp or adaptable lift.
Ability or Religion	Make Happy Hour or work parties optional.
Language	Offer interpreter services.
Race	Develop anti-racist policies.
Nationality	Remove names from resumes or applications.

Seeing Imaginary Cards Reveals Privilege

I am sure you have heard phrases like "race card," "gender card," or "disability card," flippantly tossed out to dismiss someone else's perspective, as in "Oh, they're just playing the race card." When we neglect to listen to others' perspectives, we are acting dismissively, and such gaslighting hurts the people we should be serving. When we listen and hear, we understand what the speaker is trying to say. Leaders need to listen with empathy and observe diligently what's happening around them. Some things are easy to miss without attention and care.

Start by intentionally wanting to know more about every member of your team. Acknowledge that your particular brand of privilege, from race to gender to ability, may have blinded you to things going on in your workplace. Just because you cannot (yet) see it doesn't mean it isn't happening. Practicing inclusion takes work and time. Indeed, it is a practice. A sense of belonging will only happen if people feel seen, heard, and valued.

Get Used to Discomfort

We understand that we all have biases—all of us—and when unmanaged, these biases can harm our employees, teams, and students and damage our workplace culture. It's easy to react critically, defensively, and judgmentally when we are challenged with new information or differences that make us feel uncomfortable. It's common to react defensively when we are reminded that we have biases! Instead of reacting, let us challenge ourselves to get curious. Ask one more question. Eye-opening conversations arise when we ask with curiosity and listen with empathy. Some of those may be difficult and painful. However, these lead to growth and progress when we approach them in transparency, honesty, and vulnerability. Remember that we cannot solve a problem we don't know we have. We cannot improve something without practicing. Therefore, we need to acknowledge the uncomfortable feelings and emotions to be self-aware of our responses. We need to practice both comfortable and awkward conversations because the outcome is improved communication, understanding of others' perspectives, and lasting relationships.

If every leader was to demonstrate empathy and courage, show mercy and grace in their feedback, and serve with unconditional cultural acceptance, we would avoid dehumanizing others. We must be open to knowing we don't know everything. We must be open to accepting that we can and must learn, always.

To cultivate a sense of belonging, listen to your team, identify their needs, and offer resources to meet them. Develop healthy interactions and relationships. Fine-tune your communication skills. Lead in a way that people want to follow you and listen in a way that people want to speak to you. Use cultural humility to help you understand people better, ask questions, and as you listen, stay open to learning. Be the leader who notices outdated discriminatory practices, activates and champions change and adapts to make everyone feel safe, secure, and supported.

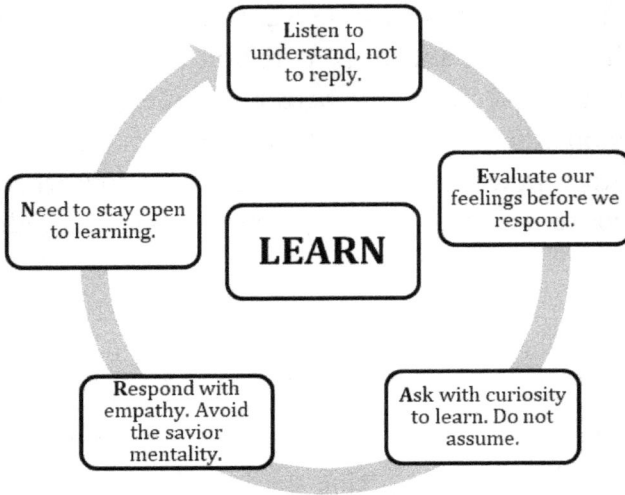

Listen to understand, not to reply.

Evaluate our feelings before we respond.

Need to stay open to learning.

LEARN

Respond with empathy. Avoid the savior mentality.

Ask with curiosity to learn. Do not assume.

TAKEAWAYS

- Notice
- Demystify
- Evolve

CALL TO LEARN

- Identify outdated discriminatory policies or practices and address them.
- Extend opportunities based on the idea of culture "add" instead of culture "fit."

MISTAKE #11

I do not like conflict;
I just want to do my job
and go home.

PRACTICE

11

Be an Agent of Change

There comes a point where we need to stop just pulling people out of the river. We need to go upstream and find out why they're falling in.
—Desmond Tutu

Change

We already know that culture and language evolve. The work of diversity, equity, and inclusion requires that we change. Change is challenging. Change is inevitable. Change is uncomfortable but necessary. Change takes time. In some cases, a few change agents live long enough to witness the outcomes of the change they fought for. When it comes to the work of DEIB, a change agent is someone who recognizes the past and the dangers of history if it were to be repeated, acknowledges the need for change, promotes and agitates to bring the needed change. Change can take years, and most times, agents of change are long gone before the intended change happens. In the words of Warren Buffet, "Someone is sitting in the shade today because someone planted a tree a long time ago." I believe that great change agents are legacy-focused, not just resume-focused. This means that effective agents of change are committed to agitating and taking action to bring the change they envision, even if this happens long after they are gone.

When I think of agents of change, I think of my grandmother, Baba Kwamboka.

A Grassroots Story, Literally

Growing up with gender inequality, as a young girl, Baba was pulled out of school and forced into an arranged marriage. After begging her father and asking her brothers to plead her case in vain, she took matters into her own hands because she knew her life and future depended on her decision and action. During the cultural bride price negotiations, she didn't show any signs of resistance even though her heart and mind were against it all. She was married off as the fifth wife to an elderly and wealthy man.

When the wedding night came, she was expected to join her husband in her new hut. Just before joining him in bed, she asked to go use the bathroom. There was no bathroom or even an outhouse. This meant going outside and hiding in a bush to relieve herself. It was not unusual to encounter wild animals who came out at night to find prey.

As soon as Baba got outside, she took off running into the darkness. She could not see anything, but she kept running. She ran further and further away, the grass scraping at her feet and legs. She ran like crazy because her fear of being a fifth wife was greater than that of being eaten by a lion or leopard. It is interesting how for a young girl, she was inspired by self-conviction and determined that this arranged marriage felt wrong. She just needed to get as far away as possible from this man. She didn't care about becoming an easy dinner for the animals as long as she didn't end up as a fifth wife to a man old enough to be her father.

In those days, the 1930s, there were all kinds of wild animals roaming freely near residential homes looking for prey. Baba was an easy and delicious meal running head-long into a hyena's claws or a lion's jaws. She finally made it home. She hid in her stepmother's house until her husband and father gave up, thinking she had been eaten by the wild animals. Eventually, Baba was allowed to return to her home, her mother's house. Her father returned the dowry, which meant she was no longer a wife. She was allowed to attend school for a couple years. Her brothers continued their education and when they became adults, they received an inheritance that included their sister's dowry paid by my grandfather.

Listening to her stories, Baba was born into a rich home to a wealthy father who wanted the best for his children according to cultural norms. After realizing that girls can be educated and do not need to be married off, she was determined to break every barrier, fight every obstacle, and live through every calamity to give her children, both boys and girls, equal opportunities. I was fortunate to be raised by such a strong grandmother who stood against gender inequality and believed in education as a means to fairness and freedom. She detested and advocated against arranged marriage by the way she lived. She sought and extended the same opportunities to all her kids and the village at large.

Despite living in a society where the cultural norm was that girls were to be seen, not heard, Baba advocated for her girls by giving them educational opportunities, advocating against arranged marriages, and teaching women how to be self-reliant. My illiterate Baba's strong faith, guidance through discipline, and support for education shaped my character and, by extension, influenced my leadership style and my belief that anyone with conviction and determination can be an agent of change. My Baba learned that what she wanted was important and her success in life depended on fighting for it. She protested her arranged marriage, fought gender inequality, embraced education, and believed in the power of bringing change, even if it meant standing alone. Later, she met, fell in love with, and married my grandfather.

Our American Stories

Charlene Teters is a well-known artist and educator of the Native American Spokane Tribe. She made the community understand why using Native American mascots is inappropriate. She took on the fight to make the universities recognize that using mascots to represent chiefs was dehumanizing to her culture. It was a lonely path that took time. Some people attacked her. Some threw soda cans or debris at her during her protests at sporting events. Some people resisted. Later she only got partial support. Eventually, more people joined her in her fight. Charlene Teters was not only a great educator and activist but a great agent of change.

In pursuing a path of inclusion, there will be resistance and even unfair punishment. We have great agents of change like Nelson Mandela, who spent 27 years in prison and never stopped fighting apartheid in South Africa until freedom came for all. We have Rosa Parks, who was sick and tired of being sick and tired when she decided to longer sit in the back of that bus. I think of great educators like James Baldwin, who once said, "It is your responsibility to change the society if you think of yourself as an educated person." I am reminded of Dr. Martin Luther King Jr., who was a pioneer in the civil rights movement in the United States and died for his vision and activism. We are beneficiaries of that legacy: To create a world where we are judged not by the color of our skin but by our character. I am a beneficiary and professionally indebted to Dr. Mary Elizabeth Carnegie, a nurse educator who advocated for quality education and full recognition of African American nurses.

To bring such significant changes took courage, sacrifice, and conviction to build a more inclusive world for others.

We, too, must focus on our legacy, not just on our resume, to create a sense of belonging for all those we serve. I hope that we will continue to apply inclusive practices so we can listen better and learn more to elevate the humanity of all. We must continue to fight and advocate for justice until what is right and just becomes the cultural norm. Even though it will take time, we must intentionally work on creating the change we want.

Agents of Change Agitate for Action

To be an agent of change, you will need crazy determination, the conviction of your vision, and the need to bring justice. There are people who are going to be completely against being inclusive. We have those who will resist changing the status quo and will argue, why change when we have always done things this way? We have others who do not have the courage to act because they are afraid of losing their jobs or offending others. I suggest we reflect on the current situation. Once we identify the problem, we then should think or envision the change we want. We should always aim to find allies and reach out to as many people who have succeeded as possible to learn how they did it. We must also pay attention to those who have tried and failed so we can avoid mistakes and save time. Sometimes, we may have to act alone because of resistance or no support. The goal of this effort for change is to remove and prevent harm, create an equitable and inclusive culture, and ensure that everyone's humanity is valued, and each person feels safe, secure, and supported.

If we are ready to learn, then:

- Start by acknowledging that we need to have conversations, especially difficult ones.

- If we feel comfortable and want to contribute, we must do so with grace and humility extended to every-one involved.
- If we are not ready to contribute yet, know that is okay. It is good to be quiet and listen.
- If we want to learn, then we must truly listen and not wait to reply.
- Once we learn, then we can take action. Implement actionable ideas with guidance to achieve the changes we seek.
- When we achieve a goal or implement a change, we should solicit feedback from our team about whether this has improved inclusion and given them a sense of belonging.

Change Creates Cultures of Belonging

Unfortunately, one meeting, one focus group, or one committee will not bring a team a sense of belonging. Hiring a diversity of-ficer and implementing a few action items will not change the company's equity, inclusion and belonging outlook. DEIB work requires fairy godmother-mentors and prince-leaders who are courageous enough to give everyone an opportunity.

Keep in mind that "including" people by hiring them but then not listening to them is making them seen but not heard. Offering them a seat at the table but drowning them out of the conver-sation is another example of seen but not heard. Implementing their ideas but not giving them credit is stealing. Leading with cultural humility allows you to listen and identify the needs of the marginalized in your organizations. Only they know what they truly need. When they share their experiences and ideas, we must be open to learning, no matter how unreal they seem or how shocking they may be. Just because we have not or do not experience something doesn't make it not true. Ask with curiosity, listen with empathy, and be willing to learn and support them. Let us be leaders who agitate and create change even when it seems far-fetched. Change to cultivate cultures of belonging is a lifelong practice.

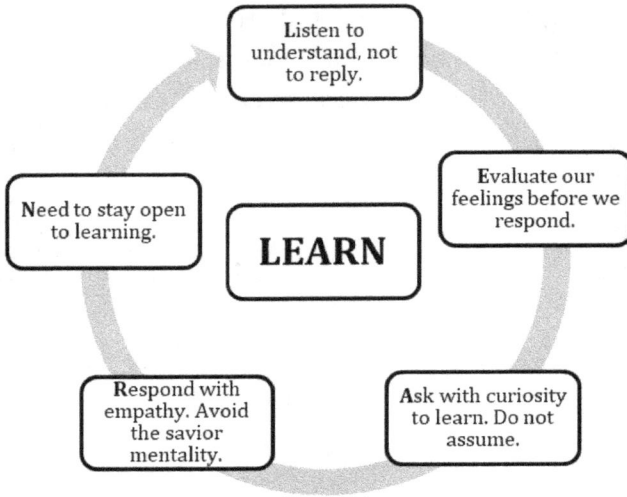

TAKEAWAYS

- To achieve DEIB, leaders must be agents of change.
- You will need courage to agitate.

CALL TO LEARN

- What are some unfair practices in your organization that could be changed to be more inclusive?
- How important is this change to you and the people you are trying to impact?

MISTAKE #12

I am ready to give up because nothing seems to work.

12

Practice Empathy and Track Your DEIB Progress

When you know the beginning well, the end will not trouble you.
—African Proverb

Managing Biases Is a Lifelong Practice

I just attended a global conference in Boston, Massachusetts, for financial professionals from 70 countries. I was interested in how they were addressing DEIB. The hotels had braille written just below the room numbers. Upon checking in at the event registration, I was given a rundown on what to expect, then the lady handed me a small brown box. She explained that that was a radio for interpretation because there were many speakers who spoke different languages from around the world. Right then, my bias was checked because I had not thought about the speakers or the possibility of needing an interpreter, even as a DEIB leader and multilingual speaker. There were elevators, escalators, stairs, several walkways, and ramps.

There were several sessions to attend. I went to one of the main events with over 5000 attendees. I was early enough so I could get comfortable and ready to welcome the speaker. They say you will find what you are looking for. Guess what? The speaker was introduced and ready to address the audience. In Korean. Remember that radio we were given at registration? I had thrown it into my purse and forgotten about it. I am used to offering interpreter services to non-English speakers, not the other way around. I quickly got my radio as I struggled to find the channel that translated to English. It took me a few minutes to catch up and follow the speaker, who had a great message for us all. This situation made me check my own biases and assumptions. It made me think of the non-English speakers whom we often expect to prepare and adapt to our majority English-speaking country. More importantly, I hope leaders recognize that minoritized people who deviate from our workplace or societal norms have to do extra work to accommodate the majority. They are given the responsibility of finding coping skills or adaptive devices to fit with the rest of the world. This is the case with any marginalized group centered on our differences such as race, gender, ability, language or even nationality.

As a leader, I got a great opportunity to be empathetic. I thought of the many times I offered interpreter services to my clients and how, at times, that inconvenienced our timed processes. This reminds us to be patient and offer people equitable resources so they can feel included.

Here are some simple actions we can offer to promote inclusion and engagement at our events:

- Tried and tested captions on a virtual meeting, video. or presentation.
- Radios with multiple language-accessible channels.
- Braille or use of sign language.
- Wheelchair-accessible escalators, elevators, or ramps.
- Rideshare or ride-buddies to accommodate the visually or hearing impaired.
- Vegetarian or vegan options on our menus.
- Non-alcoholic beverages at networking events.

The beautiful thing about diversity, equity, inclusion, and belonging is that it is a lifelong journey of learning and practicing to make people feel seen, heard, and valued. When people feel included, they will be more engaged and willing to share their ideas. It is not just nice but necessary to practice leadership with empathy so we can experience the benefits of inclusion.

Do Not Give Up. Persist. Then Assist.

While at lunch, I shared my experience above and told my friend and colleague, Dr. P., about a cultural humility workshop project I was working on. After expressing her excitement, she offered to tell me about her experience at her first job at an outpatient pharmacy:

I worked two jobs, 2nd and 3rd shifts, while going to school. You remember that. I had to pay my tuition, bills, and don't forget, send money home (Kenya). I was just moving like an automated robot. Let me tell you, students can be brutal. Whenever I wanted to contribute in class, all I heard was, "What did she say?" Initially, whenever the instructor asked us to get into groups, they didn't want me to join their groups, and no one wanted to be in groups with me. I knew I was smart but stuff like this crushes your confidence. I was so busy that my only solution was to check in with my teachers in case I needed any help. For my individual work, I got straight As. Whenever I ended up in groups, we barely made a B. It was an average outcome. I hated being in groups as much as they hated having me there. But you know what? It is ironic that some of these classmates did not make it to pharmacy school and I am the one who not only graduated with honors but got into my dream med school.

Passing my board exam is a story for another day. But listen! I was extremely proud and grateful to get my first job. Automatically, you are the leader in charge at the pharmacy. You were assigned with a pharmacy technician and that is it. I remember this one tech who literally hated me. She would tell patients that I'm new and if they have any concerns, they should tell her. She was a smoker, so she took several "smoke breaks" during work. But when I took my lunch, she set the timer. I remember one time I got a call that my sister had a medical emergency. This made me about three minutes late in reporting back. I know because I looked at the timer! As soon as I showed up, the tech yelled at me and scolded me. I didn't even have a chance to tell her my sister had an emergency. As a matter of fact, she was so loud that the customers heard her. I called my director who came in promptly to relieve me. Would you believe this tech told my director that I was lying? She told the director I had no emergency. I just wanted time off to go party with my friends like "they all do." She was rude and cruel to me especially.

I am grateful for my director. When I brought up my concerns, this tech cried and said, "I am so sorry, I am overwhelmed. She (referring to me) is the first Black person I have ever worked with." It is as though she was blaming me for being Black. Or it was my fault for getting a job there. I know her actions and my director's not doing anything about it affected my mental state. That tech had been there so long and I saw many people come and go. Yet she stayed. One day, I saw her humiliating a new tech I had hired. I could no longer sit quietly. I knew I had to change that culture. I privately met with the director and mentioned that our inaction was perpetuating that tech's inappropriate behavior. You know what? After that meeting, the tech was told to correct her behavior or leave. She quit. Since then, I started a mentorship program at that location because I never want to see anyone going through what I went through. I recently learned that it is now an active company-wide program.

Obviously, my friend is amazing! There is no one size fits all approach to DEIB work. Some interventions work at first try while others take time and at times, they do not work at all. I admire leaders like Dr. P for their resilience and creating the change they want. There are many benefits to providing and encouraging cross-generational collaboration through mentor-mentee relationships. This not only builds relationships but also improves communication and innovation.

You Cannot Measure What You Do Not Track

If you have read this book thus far, you may be able to identify some patterns when it comes to leading with cultural humility to cultivate cultures of belonging. Essentially this means intentionally practicing inclusive leadership as a lifelong process that starts with reflection, self-awareness, and taking actions that positively impact humanity. It also means training leaders to detect and mitigate conscious and unconscious biases during any human interaction. We must take necessary steps to check our assumptions and track our progress to determine if our initiatives are effective. There are many ways to measure and track our DEIB progress. I have heard many leaders complain that they do not see any results after spending millions on DEIB work. My question is, how are you tracking your work? Because you cannot measure what you do not track. While use of artificial intelligence tools is an option, we must be aware that these can have biases built into them.

A few years ago, I watched a viral video about the soap dispenser that could not recognize the hands of a user, a Black man. The man who posted the video said he tried like 10 soap dispensers in that same bathroom, but none worked. The solution. He had to get a friend, a White man, to accompany him to the bathroom every time he had to use the bathroom. He narrated that the soap dispenser worked just fine for his friend. When the engineer's bias was exposed by the software and soap dispenser, they had to revisit the process with people with dark skin tones. Since then, there have been many companies who have had discriminatory or biased software and technology. Biases can be built into tools, assessments, and equipment. This shows and reaffirms the need to train people how to detect and mitigate biases. We have a responsibility to check and detect biases so we may avoid costly mistakes, save resources and company reputations, and promote inclusion and belonging.

In recent years, we have had several campaigns dedicated to creating and promoting awareness. Yet, in our school setting we have debatable exclusive environments for our neurodivergent learners. In our work setting, we continue to witness lawsuits where marginalized groups are excluded or discriminated against. The lack of resources during the current pandemic, whether in the school, work, or healthcare settings showed how society forgot the marginalized humans. Tasks such as putting on a mask which seemed easy or simple to many were not as easy for those with different abilities. The government's guidelines and recommendations for the pandemic were exclusive for the majority population. The deaf community even sued the former president's administration because there was no sign language interpreter during the pandemic's press conferences. Some may argue that it was unintentional and we were in a crisis. It still does not lessen the impact on those with hearing impairments.

We all agree that there has been some progress. We still have a lot of work to do to create inclusive environments for all. Let us lead not just with cultural competence but with cultural humility. This is how we will recognize unique individuals and meet their unique needs. This is how we will achieve equity and respect for all humans as equals. Starting and serving with inclusion saves time, money, and resources while making sure all people feel safe, secure, and supported. Measuring your progress requires your track your process.

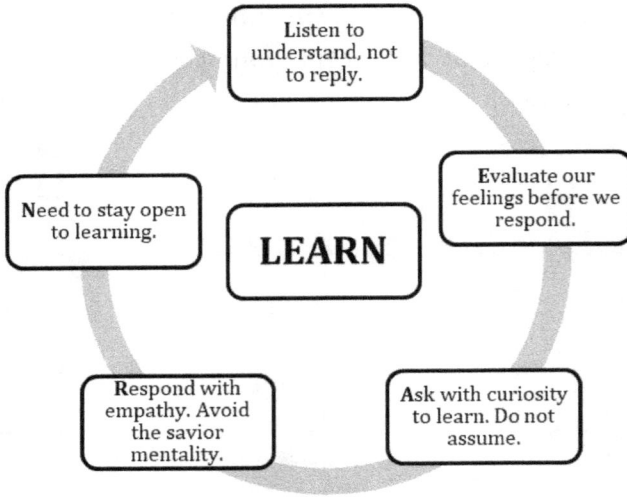

TAKEAWAYS

- You cannot effectively measure what you do not track.
- Leading with empathy builds cultures of belonging.

CALL TO LEARN

- Set a DEIB initiative, track and measure your progress.

Conclusion

I n a perfect world, we could avoid all mistakes and eliminate all biases. Unfortunately, the world isn't perfect, and improving it takes hard work. Reading one book, attending one conference, or completing a required module is only a start. It will take much more than a vision statement, hiring a diversity and inclusion officer, or mandatory seminars to manage biases and cultivate cultures of belonging. Addressing biases requires leaders to view DEIB work as a bottom-line goal, not just an optional accessory to the organization's strategic vision. Embracing diversity and creating safe and supportive spaces allows for innovative solutions and profitable impact. To become unforgettable inclusive leaders, we need cultural humility to self-reflect on our cultures and backgrounds and to remain lifelong learners who meet the needs of those we serve.

To evolve and adapt, think about your own beliefs over your lifetime. How have your beliefs changed from 5, 10, 15, 20, 30, 40, 50, or even 60 years ago? What was your view about a particular race then, and what is it now? What was your take on mental illness then, and what is it today? What was your view on neurodiversity and what is it now? What was your perspective on poverty then, and what is it now? Your attitude has probably shifted over time. There are always new perspectives, ideas, and knowledge. Language and culture evolve. People change. We need grace and to extend the same to others to recognize the changes and interrupt any biases that may surface. It is important to remember that our biases have real-life consequences that hurt people by denying their humanity and, by extension, the opportunity to live to their fullest potential, including our own.

There is danger in thinking we know everything. In assuming that people would like be treated like you. It leads to minimizing issues and the needs of others because we center ourselves. When we normalize not knowing everything and ask one more question to understand, we empathize with others and avoid assumptions. Listening to others and asking them how they prefer to be treated, maximizes their humanity. I hope you will embrace cultural humility and develop the necessary skills to improve communication and build lasting relationships.

To some of us, the DEIB work may still seem like an inconvenience, a trend, or just a passing glance. Some may see diversity as an easy box to check. We know, that until we start treating DEIB work like the big fish, an essential part of company vision, we will continue doing things the same way, expecting different results. Inclusive leaders recognize that DEIB work is not a project to be fixed or completed. It is a rewarding journey that requires time, effort, and intentional commitment because it not only affects the livelihood of marginalized and minoritized groups but it also is a profitable venture.

Now that we know that our attitudes, beliefs, and biases affect our actions and decisions, let us become agents of change so we can mitigate the effects of biases to make the marginalized feel safe, secure, and supported.

I hope this book has given you applicable resources and inspiration to create a culture of belonging in your organization. Let's go upstream and reflect on our positions in our society to manage our biases so we can leave the world better than we found it. We must do this as an investment in an inclusive world for future generations. Leading with cultural humility by applying the ideas and practices discussed here will save money, enhance communication, and build cultures where people feel safe and supported. It will build legacy leadership, worthy of emulation, where everyone feels seen, heard, and valued.

Notes

12 Mistakes Leaders Make and Can Avoid in Matters DEIB to Save Millions of Dollars

1. **I don't have biases.**

   Biases are human. We just need to manage them because unmanaged biases cause harm.

2. **I am not privileged. I have worked hard for my stuff.**

   We all have some privilege. Let us use our power and privilege to do good and right.

3. **I believe people are too easily offended or overly sensitive.**

   Instead, listen to understand and practice inclusive communication.

4. **Why hire for diversity? I do not see color anyway.**

   Diversity without inclusion has a negative impact. Focus on inclusion.

5. **As an equal opportunity employer, our focus is equality.**

   Commit to equitable and excellence Opportunities for all.

6. **I will favor those who think like us and fit in our culture.**

   Let us be fair to all, not some. Inconsistent leadership is not inclusive.

7. **I have good intentions and that's all that matters.**

   Good intent doesn't equal good impact.

8. **I am the expert. I know everything.**

   Normalize not knowing everything. Do not assume. Ask Instead.

9. **I am afraid of saying the wrong thing.**

   Don't be afraid of saying the wrong thing. An apology is a sign of courage and strength.

10. **Why change when we have always done it this way?**

    Notice the outdated stuff, demystify the myths and evolve.

11. **I don't like conflict. I just want to do my job and go home.**

    Be an agent of change. Have the courage to create the change you want.

12. **I am ready to give up because nothing seems to work.**

    DEIB progress is a lifelong process. Practice empathy and be open to learning.

Notes

Here are some ways to mitigate the effects of biases and track your DEIB progress:

- Assess and document your leadership makeup.
- Set gender-neutral recruitment standards.
- Provide, encourage, and support women into leadership roles.
- Assess pay rates and focus on pay equality.
- Provide and encourage cross-generational collaboration through mentor-mentee relationships.
- Use blind hiring software.
- Remove names from CV or resumes or before grading assignments or selecting candidates.
- Remove pictures from CV or resumes.
- Designate an interviewing panel that includes people representing different demographics to help mitigate biases.
- Develop holistic approaches to reviewing candidates so as to recognize both their strengths and weakness.
- Challenge your first impressions and evaluate your feelings.
- Avoid the savior mentality by involving the marginalized groups when addressing DEIB work.
- Develop Culturally Appropriate Leadership and Services
- Always involve the people you are trying to impact by trusting them to set up and lead Employee Resource Groups

Notes

Inclusive Cultures Create Employee Resource Groups (ERGs)

Take these simple steps to meet the needs of your employees so they can feel safe, secure and supported.

1. Start by genuinely reaching out to your marginalized and underrepresented employees, where they are. Send out anonymous surveys.

2. Be vulnerable by letting them know you struggle with what to say or do. This is how you build rapport or trust.

3. Ask them how they honestly feel, then pause, be quiet, and listen. Survey and take notes.

4. When you feel like reacting, recognize and acknowledge those feelings, then ask one more question to learn.

5. Ask them for ideas that would give them a sense of belonging. They are the ones who know their unique ideas.

6. Plan and implement the ideas they give you by investing in a qualified DEIB consultant.

7. If you hire or promote for that role within the company, train, equip and support that DEIB leader.

8. If you utilize their ideas, give them credit. Don't claim their ideas as your own.

9. Stay open to learning and make the suggested ideas your company's bottom line.

10. Develop measurable tools to track your DEIB work's effectiveness.

11. Evaluate your results and evolve to meet the specific needs of your ERG members.

12. It is only through feedback that we can determine if we have created a sense of belonging. Remember, you cannot effectively measure what you do not track.

Sources

American Public Health Association. (2018). Addressing law enforcement violence as a public health issue. Policy 201811. https://www.apha.org/policies-and-advocacy/public-health-policy-statements/policy-database/2019/01/29/law-enforcement-violence

Association of American Medical Colleges. (2022). Unconscious bias resources for health professionals. https://www.aamc.org/about-us/equity-diversity-inclusion/unconscious-bias-training

Banks, A. (2022, January 28). Never try to save people without them participating. *Around DGHI*. https://globalhealth.duke.edu/news/never-try-save-people-without-them-participating

Benedict, C. (2015). *How we learn: The surprising truth about when, where, and why it happens.* Random House.

Bonefeld, M., & Dickhäuser, O. (2018). Grading of students' performance: Students' names, performance level, and implicit attitudes. *Frontiers in Psychology.* https://doi.org/10.3389/fpsyg.2018.00481

Freeman, H. (2013, April 9). Margaret Thatcher was no feminist. *The Guardian.* https://www.theguardian.com/commentisfree/2013/apr/09/margaret-thatcher-no-feminist

General Court. (2020, December 7). General court responds to runaway servants and slaves (1640). Responds to Runaway Servants and Slaves (1640). *Encyclopedia Virginia.* https://encyclopediavirginia.org/entries/general-court-responds-to-runaway-servants-and-slaves-1640

History.com. (2019, June 7). Idi Amin. https://www.history.com/topics/africa/idi-amin

Hook, J. N., Davis, D. E., Owen, J., Worthington Jr., E. L., & Utsey, S. O. (2013). Cultural humility: Measuring openness to culturally diverse clients. *Journal of Counseling Psychology.* https://doi:10.1037/a0032595

Karani, R. Varpio, L., May, W., Horsley, T., Chenault, J., Hughes, K., & O'Brien, B. (2017). Commentary: Racism and bias in health professions education: How educators, faculty developers, and researchers can make a difference. *Academic Medicine*, 92(11S), S1-S6 https://doi:10.1097/ACM.0000000000001928

Kendi, I. X. (2019). *How to be an antiracist.* One World Books.

Kilander, G. (2022, February 3). Houston doctor sues JPMorgan Chase claiming she was barred from cashing a $16,000 check because she is Black. *The Independent.* https://www.independent.co.uk/news/world/americas/doctor-sues-jpmorgan-chase-bank-b2006326.html

Korte, G., & Gomez, A. (2018, May 17). Trump ramps up rhetoric on undocumented immigrants: "These aren't people. These are animals." USA Today. https://www.usa today.com/story/news/politics/2018/05/16/trump-immigrants-animals-mexico -democrats-sanctuary-cities/617252002/

McIntosh, P. (1989). White privilege: Unpacking the invisible knapsack. *Peace and Freedom*. https://psychology.umbc.edu/files/2016/10/White-Privilege_McIntosh-1989.pdf

McNair, T. B., Albertine, S., Cooper, M. A., McDonald, N., & Major, Jr. T. (2016). *Becoming a student-ready college: A new culture of leadership for student success*. Jossey -Bass.

National Education Association. (n.d.). Interview: Charlene Teters on Native American symbols as mascots. [Interview]. https://www.nea.org/assets/img/Pub ThoughtAndAction/TAA_00Sum_11.pdf

Norlian, A. (2020, October 9). How the deaf community challenged the White House—and won. https://www.forbes.com/sites/allisonnorlian/2020/10/09/how -the-deaf-community-challenged-the-white-houseand-won/?sh=586e3bb54243

Oxford English Dictionary. (2022). Privilege. https://www.oxfordlearnersdictionaries .com/us/definition/english/privilege_1#:~:text=privilege-,noun,or%20group%20 of%20people%20has

Penn State University. (2018). Heard on campus: Charlene Teters of the Institute of American Indian Arts. https://news.psu.edu/story/518296/2018/04/24/campus-life/ heard-campuscharlene-teters-institute-american-indian-arts

Plenke, M. (2015). The reason this "racist soap dispenser" doesn't work on Black skin. *Mic*. https://www.mic.com/articles/124899/the-reason-this-racist-soap -dispenser-doesn-t-work-on-black-skin

Quinn, D. M. (2020). Experimental evidence on teachers' racial bias in student evalu- ation: The role of grading scales. *Educational Evaluation and Policy Analysis, 42*(3), 375–392. https://doi.org/10.3102/0162373720932188

Ross, H. (2008, August). Proven strategies for addressing unconscious bias in the workplace. *CDO Insights, 2*(5). https://www.cookross.com/docs/UnconsciousBias. pdf

Rothman, L. (2016, September 16). This is how the whole birther thing started. *Time .com*. https://time.com/4496792/birther-rumor-started/

Simpson, H. (1997). Paid personal, funeral, jury duty, and military leave: Highlights from the employee benefits survey, 1979-1995. *Compensation and Working Con- ditions*. https://www.bls.gov/opub/mlr/cwc/paid-personal-funeral-jury-duty-and -military-leave-highlights-from-the-employee-benefit-survey-1979-95.pdf

Shahani-Dening, C. (2003). Physical attractiveness bias in hiring: What is beautiful is good. *Horizons*. https://www.hofstra.edu/pdf/orsp_shahani-denning_spring03.pdf

Staats, C. (2016) Understanding implicit bias: What educators should know. *American Educator, 39*(4), 29–33. https://files.eric.ed.gov/fulltext/EJ1086492.pdf

Tervalon, M., & Murray-García, J. (1998). Cultural humility versus cultural compe- tence: A critical distinction in defining physician training outcomes in multicul- tural education. *Journal of Health Care for the Poor and Underserved 9*(2), 117-125. https://doi:10.1353/hpu.2010.0233

Vanderbilt University Human Resources. Unconscious bias. https://www.vanderbilt .edu/work-at-vanderbilt/diversitytraining/ucb.php

Acknowledgements

I would like to thank all the workshop participants, students, mentees, colleagues and peers, who kept asking for a cultural humility resource. I would like to thank all the people, fans and followers that I do not know but were rooting for me to offer a resource. Thank you for challenging and inspiring me to write this book.

Thank you to my amazing book team who made this book possible. Thank you to Tri for your patience and cover designing skills. Thank you Mayfly publishing for sharing your designing talent to bring out my book. Thank you to my developmental editor, Ann Maynard, for gracefully taking my ideas and developing them. Thank you to Dr. Jessica Sipos, PhD, for your genius, patience and extraordinary editing skills. This book wouldn't be without you.

Thank you to my late Baba, who was born colonized yet survived and thrived despite the gender inequalities. Thank you for teaching me that nothing can deter a determined mind and that the simplest action of kindness can soften the hardest of hearts. I am grateful for your timeless wisdom which inspires me every day.

Thank you to all those who were before us and have left a leadership legacy worth emulating. Dr. Martin Luther King Jr, Malcolm X, Nelson Mandela, Mother Theresa, Harriet Tubman, Frederick Douglass, James Baldwin, Mary Eliza Mahoney, Mary Jane McLeod Bethune, Charlene Teters, Toni Morrison, Maya Angelou, Bell Hook, Wangari Mathai, Ngugi Wa Thiongo, Chinua

Achebe, Kwame Nkrumah, Omogaka Otenyo of Gusii, and my grandfather Alex Nyamwaya Nyambweke among others! I am in awe and remain inspired by your work.

I am grateful for my teachers, professors, mentors, coaches, supervisors and managers. Thank you for creating an impact, good or bad, in my life which inspired me to write this book. Thank you for embracing the fight to advance equity and inclusion in your various settings. At the writing of this book, I need to thank Patricia Sagert of Rasmussen University, Dr. Leanne Rogstad of Hennepin College, Dr. Virginia McCarthy of Augsburg University, Dr. Suzanne Lehman, St. Catherine University, Lisa Paige formerly of North Memorial Health Hospital, Dale Fagre and his leadership at the North Hennepin Community College Foundation, Pam Borton and Katy Burke of Team Women, and Dr. Ruth Staus of Metropolitan State University, for playing a key role in my leadership journey.

Thank you to my First Book Done (FBD) family for your unwavering support throughout my writing journey: Vania Swain, Dr Carl Stokes Jr, Patryce Sheppard, Roderick Jefferson, Staci Scott, and Connie Alleyne. May you continue inspiring and impacting lives in your spaces. Special thank you to Geovanni Derice, the FBD Coach and Book Doula, for being instrumental in birthing my book.

Thank you to my mama, Madam Pauline Nyaboke, the first educator I know who taught me to remain curious as a lifelong learner. Thank you for sacrificing your dreams so us kids could achieve ours. Thank you for believing in me and encouraging me to use my intelligence and privilege to do good as my Creator demands it.

Thank you to my sisters, Lola and Sarah-Linda, and uncle Calvin Nyamwaya, for being real and honest. It truly takes a village. Thank you for also being unafraid to correct me when I'm wrong. I love you for unconditionally having my back.

Thank you to my daughters, KK and Makayla, for being supportive, patient, and understanding why mommy is not available when you want to go outside to play during the writing process. I love you to infinity. May you remain kind and use your intelligence to do good in the world.

Thank you to my friend and husband, Jeremiah for believing in me and holding the family down every day. God bless you and keep you as we navigate this thing called life. I love you.

Thank you to my professor and mentor Dr. Ruth Staus of Metropolitan State University for not only believing in me but also encouraging me to serve beyond the classroom. This book would not be possible had you not introduced me to the concept of cultural humility. I am forever grateful for your mentorship.

Ultimate gratitude goes to my Almighty Creator for always showing up and out as only as He can!

Resources for you and your organization

I f you are interested in a class or workshop on managing unconscious biases, creating inclusive environments, how to start and develop a safe Employee Resource Group, recruiting, training and retaining diverse talent or customized DEIB initiatives for your organization, Lyna offers virtual, hybrid, and or in-person customized services to meet your specific goals.

To book Lyna for:

- Keynote Speaking
- Professional Development Training
- DEIB Consulting

Or for more DEIB tools and resources email directly to

lyna@boldimpactgroup.com

or visit

www.boldimpactgroup.com

If you enjoyed reading some parts or the whole book, please leave me a review on Amazon. I read every review and reviews help new readers learn more about my works.

About The Author

Lyna Nyamwaya is an award-winning registered nurse, educator, speaker, leadership coach and consultant who challenges and inspires people to create a positive impact. Formerly an administrative manager in a large Twin Cities hospital and an adjunct professor in a university, Lyna is the president and founder of the African Nurses Network Inc., a 501c3 organization for immigrant and refugee nurses, and CEO for Bold Impact Group.

She holds a Master of Education in Leadership from Concordia University Nebraska, Mini-MBA from St. Thomas University, Bachelor of Science in Nursing from Metropolitan State University and an Associate of Science in Nursing from North Hennepin Community College, Brooklyn Park, Minnesota.

Lyna serves on several boards and committees. For her work in higher education, healthcare, non-profit and corporate organizations, Lyna has been recognized with several awards including:

- National Role Model by Minority Access Inc., Washington DC
- Creative Nursing Award by Minnesota Nurses Association, St. Paul, MN

- Distinguished Alumna North Hennepin Community College, Brooklyn Park, MN
- Outstanding Student of the Year Metropolitan State University, St Paul MN
- Non-Profit Leadership Award by Voices Magazine, Brooklyn Park MN
- Finalist Outstanding Nurse of the Year Minneapolis-St Paul Magazine, MN
- Outstanding Mentor by Team Women-MN, Minneapolis, MN

Born in Kenya, Lyna currently lives with her family in Minnesota.

You can contact Lyna at:

Facebook: **Lyna Nyamwaya**

IG: **lynanyamwaya**

LinkedIn: **linkedin.com/in/lyna-nyamwaya/**

Internet: **www.boldimpactgroup.com**

www.lynanyamwaya.com/book

or

www.boldimpactgroup.com/book